POLICY HITS THE GROUND:
Participation and Equity in Environmental Policy-Making

Aarón Zazueta

WORLD RESOURCES INSTITUTE

September 1995

Library of Congress Cataloging-in-Publication Data

Zazueta, Aaron Eduardo.
    Policy hits the ground : participation and equity in environmental policy-making / Aarón Zazueta.
        p.   cm.
    Includes bibliographical references.
    ISBN 1-56973-002-4 (alk. paper)
    1. Environmental policy—Developing countries—Citizen participation.   2. Developing countries—
Population.   3. Sustainable development—Developing countries—Citizen participation.
I. Center for International Development and Environment (World Resources Institute)   II. Title.
GE190.D44Z39   1995
333.7'0525'091724—dc20   95-31634
                                                                                                                    CIP

Kathleen Courrier
Publications Director

Brooks Belford
Marketing Manager

Hyacinth Billings
Production Manager

Richard Saunier
Cover Photo

Each World Resources Institute Report represents a timely, scholarly treatment of a subject of public concern. WRI takes responsibility for choosing the study topics and guaranteeing its authors and researchers freedom of inquiry. It also solicits and responds to the guidance of advisory panels and expert reviewers. Unless otherwise stated, however, all the interpretation and findings set forth in WRI publications are those of the authors.

Contents

Acknowledgments

The author thanks the United States Agency for International Development, and especially the Environment Center of its Global Bureau, for encouragement and financial support. Additional financial support for this work has been provided by The Moriah Fund, the Charles Stewart Mott Foundation, and the Netherlands' Ministry of Foreign Affairs.

Special thanks are due to Patricia Ardila, whose penetrating insights helped shape this report and whose fine editing honed every line. Among other WRI colleagues who provided insightful critiques are Tom Fox, Walter Arensberg, Jonathan Lash, Walt Reid, Janet Brown, Ann Thrupp, and Bruce Cabarle. Similar expertise was shared by reviewers outside of WRI, especially Alfonso González, Michael Foley, Cristían Samper, Carlos Fonseca, and David Bray.

I am also indebted to Ilen Zazueta, Julio Vega, and Maura Paternoster for assisting with research and to Kathleen Courrier and Hyacinth Billings for shepherding this report into print.

The author thanks all of these colleagues for their contributions, but assumes full responsibility for any error or omission.

_A.Z._

Foreword

Several trends have come together to make "participation" the watchword of development policy-making for the 1990s. In most developing countries, government's role is diminishing, environmental problems are mounting, and citizens are pressing for democratic reforms. More and more, grassroots groups and non-governmental organizations are trying to meet the economic and social needs that governments have been unable to meet and to give ordinary people more of a say in plans that affect their lives. Wider participation is not just a political solution: studies by the World Bank show that development projects that local people help to design and carry out tend to work better than traditional top-down projects do. The policies and projects most likely to succeed are those that invite input from key stakeholders, including traditionally excluded groups.

The word *participation* may be common parlance, but research on how to make the concept work in real life is scarce. For this reason, *Policy Hits the Ground: Participation and Equity in Environmental Policy-making* by Dr. Aarón Zazueta, director of the Latin America program in WRI's Center for International Development and Environment, should excite debate. Leaving theory largely to others, Dr. Zazueta writes from experience—his own and that of other Latin American development practitioners. He also breaks rank with activists who idolize the wisdom of "the people" and recognizes that oppression does not in itself confer moral superiority: the villagers, peasants, indigenous communities, or women

who gain a seat at the table under the rubric of "participation" are sometimes right and sometimes wrong when it comes to solving environmental problems. The key is to create a process that gathers, recognizes, and tests the views and ideas of all competing interests and creates an opportunity to build understanding.

Drawing on his experience as a facilitator of participatory policy-making in many Latin American countries, Dr. Zazueta shows how to take advantage of the differing strengths of each negotiating party. At the outset, he acknowledges inherent difficulties. In any planning exercise, for instance, each party has its own interests at heart and thus tends to see another group's gain as its own loss. Dr. Zazueta details ways to diffuse tensions and help opposing parties find common ground. He also shows how facilitators can often forestall wrong turns if they have thought through the exercise ahead of time—even though the outcome of any truly participatory process cannot be foretold.

Naturally, widespread participation is easier to bring about in a small village where people know each other and all kinds of community institutions and resources can be tapped. But it can also be employed to improve national policies, as exemplified by WRI's work with PROAFT, the Mexican Program for the Protection of Tropical Forest. PROAFT involved people with greatly differing views about the country's tropical forests, including non-governmental organizations (NGOs) critical of the government. Such goals as a better life, more cash, and healthy forests were easy to articulate, but when PROAFT presented its forestry proposal to the international Tropical Forestry Action Plan roundtable, the assembled NGO representatives were reluctant to ask tough questions about the proposal. After PROAFT staffers broke the ice by pointing out a few flaws, others joined in a rousing critique, and the group soon found ways to fix the flaws. Such give and take is uncommon in Mexico, but PROAFT had worked with WRI for two years on participatory problem-solving, so it wasn't afraid to let go and see what happened. The revised proposal was the first approved by the Zedillo administration's Ministry of the Environment.

Some NGOs imagine that they can have as much of a voice in the government's final decisions as they do in the policy dialogue beforehand, but that won't happen—an important point that emerges from reading between the lines of *Policy Hits the Ground*. Yet, even though governmental decisions cannot be made by consensus, they will be better informed if officials have heard from everyone who has a stake in the matter. This insight is especially important at a time when Latin America's governments are trying to become more open and participatory and when the region's NGOs and other groups in civil society are trying to learn how to propose specific ways to improve policies instead of merely opposing their governments' existing policies.

Policy Hits the Ground supplies a wealth of detail and analysis that amplify the findings set forth in such WRI studies as *Strengthening EIA Capacity in Asia: Environmental Impact Assessment in the Philippines, Indonesia, and Sri Lanka*, *Environmental Challenges in Latin America: Building Organizational Capacities*, *Movers and Shapers: NGOs in International Affairs*, and *Engendering Central American Forestry Management: The Integration of Women in Forest Policy Initiatives*.

We would like to thank the United States Agency for International Development, the Netherlands Ministry of Foreign Affairs, the United States Department of Agriculture Forest Service, the Moriah Fund, the Charles Stewart Mott Foundation, and the Botwinick-Wolfensohn Foundation for their financial support of the work described in *Policy Hits the Ground*. To all six, we are deeply grateful.

Jonathan Lash
President
World Resources Institute

Introduction

A notion has evolved over the last decade that Earth's environment must be protected to maintain its capacity to meet the needs and aspirations of current and future generations. Called sustainable development, this notion has gained worldwide acceptance, and it has some very practical policy-making applications. It means sound environmental management, broad-based economic development, and the equitable distribution of goods and services. But these three components of sustainable development cannot be realized unless democratization continues and all sectors of society are included in bargaining over resource use, allocation, and distribution.

The end of the Cold War held two clear lessons. One is that centrally controlled economic systems do not generate wealth for all nor equally distribute it among all people. The second is that when the market goes unchecked, individuals use their natural resources short-sightedly, enticed by short-term benefits and heedless of the needs of both marginal populations and future generations. Ironically, the social and environmental consequences of these diametrically opposed approaches are remarkably similar: poverty, resource depletion, and environmental degradation.

The link between democratic participation, poverty alleviation, and improved environmental management is based on three assumptions. First, if ways to involve marginal populations in policy-making are found, projects and programs will better respond to their needs. Second, it is in the interest of these populations to support policies and projects that will directly improve environmental management since they bear a disproportionate share of the costs of environmental degradation and since better management will often improve their living conditions. And, third, once people's basic needs are met, they will be more willing to invest in the well-being of future generations.

This document provides operational concepts and methodological guidelines for getting "stakeholders" to participate productively in environmental policy-making through policy dialogue, as well as examples of how it is done. Clearly, all the citizens of a nation have some stake in policies, projects, or other governmental actions and their outcomes. But since it is our purpose here to explore and show how decision-making and implementation can be made more equitable and democratic, this report will focus on how to incorporate groups that have traditionally been unfairly excluded from the decision-making process—the poor, minorities, women, and other disadvantaged groups.

Chapter One describes the conditions leading to an unprecedented opportunity for policy dialogue on sustainable development with high stakeholder participation. Chapter Two assesses the potential benefits of participation and shows how to minimize its inherent costs and risks. Chapter Three describes the changes that environmental policy-making agencies in government are undergoing; it characterizes the organizations of the civil society that now take part in environ-

1

mental policy dialogue—or could—and provides guidelines on how government agencies can enlarge stakeholder participation in this dialogue. Based on concrete examples, the final Chapter provides recommendations on how governments, donor agencies, non-governmental organizations (NGOs), and other agents of change can help strengthen the capacities of stakeholders' organizations to participate more effectively in policy dialogue and policy-making.

By and large, the concepts, guidelines, and examples found here spring from the World Resources Institute's experiences with participatory environmental projects, mainly in Latin America. In a few cases, thoroughly documented case studies from other sources have been used to press a point. In this sense, this study is not intended to be comprehensive or to impart the last word on how participation should take place in environmental policy-making. Rather, it is an attempt to share with both government agencies and independent organizations the concrete results of, and the lessons learned from, various types of participatory experiences. Since these processes are highly dynamic, however, readers should be sure to place the following accounts within the time-frame documented here. The hope is that government agencies, donors, and non-governmental and grassroots organizations will use these experiences as a reference, a source of inspiration, or a starting point as they search for new and creative ways to involve stakeholders in environmental policy-making.

I. An Historic Opportunity For Increasing Participation

An unusual opportunity has emerged in developing countries over the last decade to foster participatory democracies, address important environmental problems, and build more equitable societies. Governments are increasingly finding themselves under pressure from their own citizenry—through non-governmental and grassroots organizations—and the international community—through development agencies and multilateral bodies—to open up and increase the channels or mechanisms for participation. This is good news for sustainable development because, if correctly used, this opportunity can enhance equity by including the interests of the poor in decision-making. Because the poor are increasingly making environmental degradation a central issue, their participation in policy-making can be an important tool for expanding constituencies that support improved environmental management.

A. Sanctioning Popular Participation

Increasingly, governments worldwide have been accepting sustainable development as a framework for defining economic policy. Key to sustainable development is the participation of stakeholders in bargaining over resource use, allocation, and distribution (Zazueta, 1993). Therefore, decision-makers at many levels of government have been gradually involving a variety of interest groups in policy-making processes affecting natural resource planning and management.

Mutual interests and mutual responsibilities form the basis of this structured participation. International governmental bodies such as the Organization for Economic Co-operation and Development (OECD) and major multilateral institutions, such as the World Bank, the Inter-American Development Bank (IDB), and the Asian Development Bank, have lately established procedures for assessing the environmental and social impacts of their development-assistance activities, especially on marginal populations—including ethnic minorities, the poor, and women—who up until now have been largely excluded from the benefits of development (OECD, 1991; World Bank, 1992; Freeman, 1991). These new procedures seek to incorporate citizen participation in decision-making to ensure that environmental and social factors are properly considered in economic cooperation. Coupled with growing national constituencies for the environment, these new policies have prompted most developing nations to begin integrating environmental and social concerns into national development planning. One hundred and thirty-five countries have published national environmental reports compiled with technical and financial assistance from international development agencies (WRI, 1993). Environmental impact assessments of development projects—for which the borrower nation is now responsible—have become a condition for economic cooperation (World Bank, 1992a; Freeman, 1991; OECD, 1991).

Some countries, seeking to comply with donors' conditions, have made participation part of development planning. With mixed results, the Mexican government has occasionally increased participation in an attempt to accommodate growing civil discontent with extreme poverty and the political system (Moguel, 1990). For example, the new law of the environment (1988) and the new forestry law (1993) require the establishment of regional and national advisory committees and certain participatory mechanisms as means to ensure permanent dialogue during policy formulation and implementation (SEDESOL, 1993). In Central America, the end of the Cold War and the "communist threat" strikes many as an opportunity to build democratic structures and broaden the basis of policymaking. In Colombia, the New National Constitution and its regulatory framework, issued in 1991, have institutionalized numerous forms of citizen participation and expression, such as "popular actions," "open councils," and "popular consultations," some of which citizens groups have already used. In Bolivia, the Law of Public Participation (1994) has brought about two important changes. First, by altering the way local officials are elected, it provides more opportunities for rural populations to affect the outcome of municipal elections. Second, by creating local development organizations and by broadening the taxing powers of local governments, it seeks to funnel economic resources toward municipalities. In the first six months alone, the law increased financial resources by more than 1,000 percent in most rural municipal governments in the country (Boletín Financiero N°2, February 1995). These examples show that as pressures increase on governments to open up policy- and decision-making, and as citizens become more organized to protect their interests, the public will be better prepared to participate actively in making sustainable development a reality (WCED, 1987).

Still, the search for and implementation of more equitable and environmentally sound development strategies requires many changes. New policies are needed to steer economic activities in ways that do not harm the environment. New legislation and regulations must be enacted and enforcement capacities built if laws

and regulations are to have a significant impact. Strengthening these capacities requires training qualified decision-makers and staff—a task in which multilateral bodies and development agencies have a unique role to play. But even more important, it will require raising community awareness and gaining people's support for appropriate measures to address the most pressing issues (UNCED, 1993; World Bank, 1992a).

Most informed observers agree that such support will not be forthcoming unless groups with vested interests in policy and institutional reforms are encouraged to help design and implement projects and programs (Cernea, 1992). For this reason, participation has become the latest buzzword in the official discourse of both international development organizations and governments in many developing countries. In practice, however, its real meaning varies from using people as laborers on government-driven community development projects (Esteva, 1995; Moguel, 1990) to getting stakeholders directly involved in defining environmental policy guidelines and in designing projects and programs (PROAFT, 1994; Ramón, 1993; CCAD, 1992).

Experience in democratic societies has shown that interest groups that can influence policy frequently reap the highest benefits. It has also proven that those without the access or power needed to gather political support for their own agendas end up paying a disproportionate share of the costs incurred by policies that may not even benefit them. Clearly, influence is often a function of money and political leverage, as it is in the case of many U.S. and European lobbies. But influence can also be a function of numbers—especially if people are organized—and the poor are certainly numerous in most developing countries. And now that it is widely acknowledged that poverty stands in the way of sustainable development, decision- and policy-makers are beginning to realize that including marginal populations—not excluding them—is what gives nations the chance to pursue their development goals.

B. Linking the Environment to Human Well-Being Through Grassroots Action

Even though marginal populations (small farmers, ethnic groups, informal workers, women) all too often benefit the least from unchecked economic growth, they frequently bear a disproportionately high share of the costs of environmental degradation. Agricultural productivity drops as soils erode, both drudgery and working hours increase if only land on steep hills is available for cultivation, and economic losses and health service costs rise as disease saps labor productivity (During, 1990). Productive resources remain concentrated in the hands of the wealthy (Painter and Durham, 1995) while low-income groups become increasingly marginalized as they are relegated to rural and urban areas in which resources are fragile and living conditions are tough.

Untreated industrial and municipal discharges, the lack of safe water and sanitation facilities, inadequate housing, and environmental disasters all primarily afflict marginal populations worldwide. Some of these communities now see the link between environmental degradation and deteriorating living standards and are beginning to address environmental problems, especially in the face of state inaction. In different parts of the world, environmental action initiated at the grassroots is spreading. In the savannahs of the Brazilian Amazon, the Mêbêngokrê Indians have created forest islands and promoted biodiversity and soil fertility through sophisticated ecological engineering (Posey, 1993). In the outskirts of Mexico City, the community of San Miguel Teotongo is carrying out a demonstration project on ecologically sound technologies. By setting aside community lands for conservation and experimenting with environmentally appropriate food crops, the people of San Miguel have committed themselves to protecting the urban environment and an ecological reserve adjacent to their community (Castro and Flores, 1994). In the hills of Nepal, traditional farmers are reversing soil erosion and degradation by harvesting soil from landslides and rivers and by terracing previously barren areas (Tamang, 1993). In the Volta region in Ghana, a cooperative of local farmers has turned infertile ground into productive farmland by combining forestry and agriculture (Dorm-Adzobu et al., 1991). In Katheka, Kenya, communities of men and women have organized themselves into traditional voluntary self-help groups called "mwethyas" to fight soil erosion and resource degradation by building bench terraces, subsurface dams, and hand pumps (Slayter et al., 1991).

In many cases, the policy context is hostile to these initiatives. Property rights are unclear, the poor lack access to credit and markets, or wages and crop prices are low. In addition, rarely do either the communities themselves or the nongovernmental organizations (NGOs) that support and advise them have the technical and financial resources needed to sustain self-help. It has become increasingly obvious that governments, as well as multilateral and bilateral agencies, must help create the conditions that will make these community-based projects and programs sustainable. The three keys to success are (a) the political will to support these initiatives; (b) a policy framework that builds capacities among disadvantaged people to foster their involvement in the design and implementation of policies, programs, and projects affecting them; and (c) resources to support community efforts.

The emerging avenues of sanctioned participation are an enlightened response from government officials and other politically powerful groups to pressures by independent political organizing among the disempowered and their supporters. But sanctioned participation differs from independent political organizing among the disempowered. In sanctioned participation, the state defines the dialogue by establishing objectives, a set of rules, processes, and discussion themes, all of which are aimed at reducing conflicts and confrontations while seeking to identify consensus for action. Independent political organizing, on the other hand, tends to focus on the interests of the disempowered and might use an array of means ranging from denouncement, confrontation, or negotiation. Building such capacities to respond to and further expand emerging opportunities for sanctioned participation is key to its success.

II. The Benefits And Risks of Participation

A good understanding of the benefits and risks of participation is important to correctly assess opportunities for more democratic decision-making. On one hand, government officials must be aware of the vicissitudes and the costs inherent in both participatory and non-participatory processes so they can take precautionary measures to correct them. On the other hand, citizen groups and other institutions of civil society must also assess both the benefits and the risks of participation and realize that changes rarely occur overnight. In short, they must have realistic expectations.

By analyzing the results of non-participatory development projects around the world, comparative studies are providing increasing evidence of the importance of both building local participation and taking into account sociocultural factors affecting project design, planning, and implementation. An evaluation of 25 projects sponsored by the World Bank (1993) found that 13 of them had been discontinued a few years after financial assistance had ended. Lack of attention to participation and to local organization-building when the projects were formulated and implemented appeared to be the main cause. Another study (Kottak, 1991) showed the high costs of not incorporating social considerations into development: projects found compatible with local socioeconomic conditions were deemed more successful and showed markedly higher rates of return (18.3 percent) than those that were not (8 percent).

Success has also eluded projects that involve intended beneficiaries in implementation without seeking their input in project inception and planning. A 1982 internal World Bank review of 164 projects found that though 40 percent of them intended to transfer some aspects of implementation to beneficiaries, the latter were not included in project planning. Where communities were not consulted from the start, inaccurate assessments and information about local institutions were common. On some occasions, this false start led to the creation of unnecessary institutions or inappropriate or unworkable project proposals. Conversely, implementation was successfully delegated in projects that sought people's involvement in design and planning, were flexible about incorporating local perspectives, and built on existing institutions (Cernea, 1991).

Lack of participation can also lead affected populations to reject or fiercely oppose projects. This is especially true when government initiatives attempt to tackle problems from a panoramic perspective, while failing to consider local angles. A case in point is the construction of a dam on the Upper Balsas River in the area of San Juan Tetelcingo, in Guerrero, Mexico to halt siltation at the Caracol Dam and generate electricity for the city of Puebla's industrial area, Mexico City and Acapulco. Planned in the 1960s, the design was finalized in the mid-1980s. From an engineering standpoint, the Tetelcingo Dam represents a sound project. Yet, it is expected to displace close to 60,000 people and flood an area with many endemic species and many archeological sites.

Area residents and environmental groups learned about the project in 1990, when land-surveying brigades began measurements and access roads were opened. As more details came to light, a movement was formed by the communities, with the support of NGOs and universities, to stop construction. Negotiations between the Mexican government and the local committee,

---

Box 1. Going to Extremes

In developing countries, people's demands for participation have traditionally been either ignored or answered by state repression. Moreover, the lack of opportunities to further their interests still pushes some communities to resort to violence. Indeed, violence as a net cost—in terms of human lives, economic losses, and environmental damage—must always be accounted for when conducting a cost-benefit analysis of participation.

The bloody uprising of Indian peasants in Mexico's southern state of Chiapas in January 1994 dramatically illustrates the negative and costly impact of exclusionary, non-participatory development strategies. The rebellion started precisely when wealthier Mexicans were welcoming the New Year and the kick-off of the North American Free Trade Agreement (NAFTA), which has been promoted by former president Carlos Salinas de Gortari as the nation's ticket out of the Third World.

Nevertheless, the war declaration issued by the Ejército Zapatista de Liberación Nacional (EZLN)—formed mainly by Indian and *mestizo* peasants of Mayan descent—not only denounced NAFTA and the process of modernization that has clearly passed them by, but also the neglect, displacement, and exploitation that they have endured for more than 400 years. It is estimated that more than 50 percent of the population of Chiapas lives in poverty. Despite government promises of land redistribution, wealthy landowners have prevailed since the mid-1800s. As a result, 40 percent of the land is owned by only four percent of the people, 87 percent of the population crowds onto another 40 percent of the land, and 200,000 peasants are landless.

The area where the uprising began is an entry point to the Lacandona rainforest, a refuge for the poorest and most desperate of the landless. Over the last thirty years, an estimated 350,000 hectares of forest have been cleared in Chiapas—usually with government support—to raise cattle and grow coffee and other cash crops, activities all linked to the commercial and export markets. Subsistence farmers have thus been forced onto steep slopes, where deforestation results in heavy erosion and the loss of species is inevitable once trees are cut. As their resource base shrank and deteriorated, so did the possibilities to improve their living standards. For example, 1992 estimates on the social conditions of Las Margaritas—one focal point of the rebellion—showed that 95 percent of all peasant children were undernourished.

The Salinas administration's first reaction to the rebellion was to blame it on foreign agitators and to send in planes to bomb the area. But soon after, the government stopped the firing, declared amnesty, and acknowledged that urgent action was needed to address the social problems cited by rebel leaders as reasons for their call to arms. President Ernesto Zedillo has followed a similar path. The sudden shift from a military response to a negotiated solution indicated the government's admission not only that the insurgents' grievances had a political basis but also that the Zapatistas had rapidly gained widespread social support. These are signs that the government might be accepting the fact that it must deal with the insurgents as worthy interlocutors if it wants to find concrete solutions to the problems facing the region's inhabitants (*Houston Chronicle*, January 26, 1994; Mexico & NAFTA Report 1994, 1995; Benjamin, 1989).

formed by 22 Indian communities, were mediated by the National Indian Institute. By January 1991, facing increasing political pressure and opposition to the dam, the government of former President Salinas suspended the project indefinitely. It will be up to the current administration (1994–2000) to decide the project's final fate. Meanwhile, the Indian communities of the area have asked NGOs to help them develop a regional plan to address the siltation of Caracol Dam by means other than a new dam (CPNAB-GEA, 1993; CPNAB, 1993).

Opposition to the Tetelcingo Dam arose from unilateral planning. The responsible agency, the National Electricity Commission (CFE), did not involve the affected population in negotiations until its technical team had already defined the problem and its solution in engineering terms. Residents had no part in the problem nor in exploring different options to address it. As a result, the strategy adopted by the Indian communities was to stop the project and demand a more rigorous social and environmental impact assessment, thus creating time to find alternatives. Whether or not this impasse will give way to a dialogue in which both CFE's concern with the siltation of the Caracol Dam and the needs of the Indian communities are addressed depends largely on whether the population can broaden consensus around their alternative proposal and on how the current administration assesses the political liabilities or benefits.

These kinds of impasses, common in large government-sponsored infrastructure projects, help illustrate the importance of involving stakeholders early in planning, when the problem is first defined and alternative solutions explored. In the case of the Tetelcingo Dam, the costs of neglecting people's involvement will be paid down the road when siltation of the Caracol Dam lowers electrical outputs and brings on energy shortages in the region's cities and industrial facilities.

A. The Benefits of Participation

The core argument in favor of participation is that policy-making and implementation are more likely to succeed when stakeholders are part of the process that leads to policy decisions. The assumption is that different stakeholders will seek to bring to bear as much information as they can to support their interests, and that once "critical mass" is reached, the potential benefits and costs of the various courses of action will be analyzed. It is expected that the best decision among the available options will be taken and that this process will result in a more equitable distribution of benefits among all stakeholders.

Participation is likely to improve policy-making and implementation in three major ways:

1. It brings into decision-making more information and a wider range of experiences—both of which contribute to the elaboration of more realistic policies and projects.

2. It helps gather political support for and reduce opposition to policy proposals, projects, and other decisions by building in stakeholders' concerns.

3. It builds local capacities and makes implementation easier.

1. Expanding the Information Base for Decision-making

Increasing evidence shows that the information that people affected by projects can provide, coupled with decision-makers' ability to use it, is key to making such projects and the policies behind them work.

In the Philippines, for example, the National Irrigation Administration found that farmers provided detailed technical and sociological information that helped engineers design irrigation channels (Bagadion and Korten, 1991). Similarly, a comparative study of irrigation projects for the same agency indicated that farmers in participatory projects found their irrigation facilities more functional; they abandoned only 9 percent of the irrigation structures, compared with 18 percent in non-participatory projects (Reyes and Jopillo, 1986).

In agricultural research and extension, farmers' participation has also brought critical information to program and technology development. Combined with that developed by interdisciplinary teams, their knowledge has resulted in the creation of simple technologies that are economically and culturally compatible with small-holder farmers' needs. Such is the case with the development of the Diffuse Light Storage Technology for keeping potatoes fresh. By involving farmers in defining the problem and testing new technologies, the International Potato Center in Peru developed simple, low-cost equipment that reduced potato losses during storage. Besides allowing low-risk trials and experimentation, the technology was easy to disseminate from farmer to farmer, so extension costs were low (Rhoades and Booth, 1982).

Over the last decade, a growing body of literature has confirmed that small-farm production systems are quite complex and diversified, requiring a variety of resource-use strategies. Knowledge accumulated over centuries gives small-holder farmers a detailed understanding of soils, climate, genetic varieties of crops, and pest control. Many scientists and practitioners now believe that the knowledge of small-holder farmers is an overlooked asset that can contribute to the success of agricultural projects (Rocheleau, 1991; Chambers et al., 1990; Fujisaka, 1990; Bunch, 1989; Thrupp, 1989). This recognition has led to the development of farmer-to-farmer extension programs, that have improved farming practices and introduced cost-effective technologies. In Mexico, Adult Education Services (SEDAC) and the Heifer Project have created a revolving-loan and farmer-exchange program to improve and expand cattle production in the Valley of Mezquital, one of the country's poorest regions. Heifer usually gives loans in cattle to small farmers, which they are expected to pay back in kind (the same number of cattle of the same age). As old loans are repaid, new ones are made available. In this case, SEDAC convinced Heifer to build on the communal tradition among the Hñahñu (Otomí indians) and give calves to organized groups instead of to individuals. At farmers' meetings, participants evaluate their practices

and share useful technical information on animal health and reproduction. Then, after listening to these exchanges, technical consultants give the farmers advice. Through group management and this type of technical training, farmers have learned correct stock-insemination and birth procedures and how to keep accurate accounts on each cow (SEDAC/FFE, 1992). Held every two months since 1987, the meetings have also helped raise and address other community concerns, such as nutrition and economic well-being. The project, which started with six groups and 95 cows, now has 24 groups with 250 cows. Experiences such as SEDAC's show how external agents can incorporate technical knowledge into farmers' daily practices by drawing from and supplementing people's knowledge and abilities instead of ignoring or attempting to replace them with alien concepts and procedures.

Participation during various stages of planning can help build the stakes of all groups affected by policies or projects.

2. Building Support and Reducing Opposition to Policies and Programs

Participation during various stages of planning can help build the stakes of all groups affected by policies or projects. The case of the Tetelcingo Dam described earlier showed how lack of participation can stop a project. On the other hand, helping people better understand policies, projects, and their consequences will prompt them to identify potential negative impacts and find alternative ways to reach policy goals.

Many development programs and projects have been severely hampered by opposition from government bureaucracies, organized groups, and even from their intended beneficiaries. Large-scale projects and complex policy frameworks tend to be particularly controversial since competing agendas and interests need to be reconciled to move forward (Morss and Hondale, 1985). Internal evaluations conducted by the World Bank have found that many projects are "virtually impossible to implement because they lacked proper incentives for participation and acceptance of project goals." The first step toward addressing this problem is for the officials responsible for implementation to identify the levels and forms of involvement of the affected populations (Kottak, 1991).

Because people have to live with the consequences of policies or projects, many become suspicious when they are not given enough information to make assessments. Participation can help constituents better understand what is being proposed. It can also help both policy-makers and stakeholders explore probable consequences and proceed accordingly to prevent negative impacts.

One example of how governments can work with local populations to implement large-scale programs is the Awa Colonization program on the border of Northwestern Ecuador. In 1980, the news of a road being built in the area prompted considerable opposition from organized Indian and environmental groups concerned with the well-being of the Awa communities and possible deforestation. Responding to grassroots pressure, the government formed an inter-institutional commission on the project and invited the National Project Coordinating Council of the Indian Nations of Ecuador (CONANIE) to represent the Awa people on it. Thanks to this collaboration, Awa lands have been demarcated, citizenship cards have been issued to more than 1,100 Awa, and the governments of Ecuador and Colombia have agreed to work together in a comprehensive program to help protect the area from uncontrolled colonization.

The Awa communities have organized themselves to protect their territorial integrity by building permanent settlements and by planting fruit orchards in future entry points of the reserve *before* road construction begins (Archibold, 1992; Poole, 1989). In this case, involving groups that initially opposed the project clearly paid off.

Letting interested groups express their needs and fears and negotiate solutions acceptable to all through the inter-institutional development commission took time and required government officials to be flexible. But by allowing these groups to help design the project, the government gave Indians and environmental groups an enormous stake in it.

It will not always be possible to make all interest groups winners in policy reform or development projects.

It will not always be possible to make all interest groups winners in policy reform or development projects. Frequently there will be losers. In these instances, participation will allow officials to get a better sense of how populations are likely to be harmed by the projects and to identify measures that can help reduce detrimental impacts as well as political opposition.

3. Building Local Implementation Capacities

Participation in project implementation boosts project success in various ways. It often helps reduce costs by tapping local resources, allows timely modifications, and incorporates local organizations as support mechanisms for the project. More important, participation during implementation helps build the community's technical and organizational capacities, as well as its ability to negotiate. Progress on these fronts ensures that benefits from programs or projects will continue to flow even if outside financial and technical assistance is low (MacDonald, 1992; Poole, 1989; Van Sant, 1987; Uphoff, 1986, 1993; Korten, 1980).

The National Irrigation Administration (NIA) program in the Philippines illustrates the impact that participation can have on long-term program implementation. With financial support from the

World Bank and the Ford Foundation, the NIA carried out a seven-year participatory irrigation project involving 1,335 communities on 180,000 hectares. When the program began in 1980, it consisted of only 12 projects. By 1981, the number of projects had doubled, and the following year it reached 180. By 1983, the participatory approach became the norm for NIA community-irrigation projects. It consisted primarily of incorporating into the project full-time community organizers who worked with local farmer associations to plan, design, and construct irrigation works. Twofold benefits derived from this approach: local skills were further developed, and farmers' commitment to the project was heightened.

An evaluation comparing the NIA approach with less participatory irrigation projects in the Philippines concluded that farmers find NIA irrigation structures more acceptable since such structures respond better to their needs. These projects also helped user groups better manage and maintain irrigation systems. According to the evaluation, developing simple accounting systems with user groups in workshops increased the use of vouchers, which in turn facilitated accountability for how funds were used. Transparent systems to manage funds proved to be critical in increasing the farmers' trust in their organizations.

Similarly, workshops and community meetings helped form new leaders among small farmers involved in the projects. Management systems were more participatory as a result, and irrigation schedules were more equitably applied than in the non-participatory projects. Overall, participatory projects gave rise to stronger user organizations, which enabled NIA to decentralize irrigation management. This centrifugal force proved critical for organizing routine tasks in projects where members were geographically dispersed (Bagadion and Korten, 1991).

B. Minimizing the Costs and Risks of Participation

Participation has some real costs and risks for development activities and decision-making processes. Frequently, it will require more time and money during problem identification and project planning, thus affecting schedules and budgets. Because participation entails incorporating stakeholder interests into decisions, it can also raise expectations, not all of which can be met. It may also trigger conflicts among different stakeholders: if participation is not insured across the board, the involvement of a few can result in an unequal distribution of benefits. But such costs and risks can be effectively minimized, so they need not be an obstacle in participatory processes.

1. Factoring Time and Money

In most instances, the use of participatory approaches makes project planning slower and more expensive. In the case of the NIA in the Philippines, participatory projects took a few more months than non-participatory projects. The program had to develop and test training materials, workshop guidelines, and accounting systems so as to get people involved in these activities. Similarly, user groups had to be organized and gradually strengthened. In all instances, NIA's irrigation projects required flexibility in planning and implementation to respond to the affected populations' needs. Staff had to give up their customary ways of planning—unilateral for the most part—and learn to work as communicators, facilitators, and negotiators, all of which required training. These additional tasks raised planning costs slightly, but such increases were clearly offset during implementation. Specifically, the cost per hectare of participatory projects was only $2.40 more than in non-participatory projects. But recovery rates of equity contributions (a 10-percent capital recovery from farmers is required by Philippine law) were higher in participatory projects (82 percent) than in non-participatory projects (50 percent) (Bagadion and Korten, 1991).

In the case of the Awa reserve in Ecuador, project officials involved the various government agencies with a stake in the road/colonization project and let CONANIE represent the Awa Indians. This took time, and the original plan had to be modified to support the formation of Awa organizations that could promote the organized colonization of their territory (Poole, 1989).

In the two examples mentioned above, investment in time and money paid off. It built commitment to participate during program implementation and helped create organizations that have kept the projects functioning smoothly after initial funding and technical support ended.

2. Meeting People's Expectations

Since participation naturally builds up the stakes of affected populations in policies and projects, their expectations inevitably rise as a result. Problems may develop if people expect more than the project can possibly deliver or if what seemed to be reasonable under certain circumstances becomes increasingly difficult to attain as conditions change.

In Ecuador, for example, the NGO Sistemas de Investigación y Desarrollo Comunitario (COMUNIDEC), in collaboration with World Resources Institute, provided technical assistance to five Indian federations in the provinces of Chimborazo and Bolívar to formulate environmental management plans entailing strong participation at the village level. For this purpose, COMUNIDEC developed a micro-regional planning methodology called Andean Community Planning (PAC), which ensures high levels of involvement by villagers in all planning stages. The resulting plans were presented to international donors as part of Ecuador's Tropical Forest Action Plan (TFAP) in 1991.

However, project review and approval were slow and uncertain. After six months, the communities involved grew increasingly impatient with the pace of the process and the lack of response from international donors and demanded action from federation leaders. PAC had been so successful in motivating villagers that they were now expecting that the plans they had elaborated so carefully would be implemented at once. The situation was delicate, and without immediate action, both community leaders and COMUNIDEC would risk losing support and credibility from their constituents. COMUNIDEC could do little

to speed up the bureaucratic process; but rather than allow local leaders and the institution itself to lose popular support and credibility, COMUNIDEC, the five federations, and the World Resources Institute agreed that WRI would provide a small grant to initiate trial activities that addressed water and soil management. Over one year, COMUNIDEC worked with the federations to test technologies, carefully measuring costs and benefits. By the time the grant was approved, the program had already tested technologies that could then be adopted on a wider scale.

In this case, participatory methods both motivated the villagers and raised their expectations. But people welcomed the technological trials proposed by COMUNIDEC because they could observe the results without risking their own crops. These trials also kept the communities from questioning COMUNIDEC and the federation's capacities to deliver. Once the funds arrived and the success of the trial was clear, farmers were even more interested in participating in the project.

3. Managing Diverging Interests and Conflicts Triggered by Participation

Sooner or later, various stakeholders' interests will diverge or conflict in participatory processes. Because participation not only brings marginal groups into policy-making but also builds their capacities to voice their needs and concerns effectively, the process almost always entails changes in power relations. Those who have traditionally prevailed often resist change because a truly participatory process demands that power be progressively shared with groups traditionally excluded from bargaining. In the Philippines, the Upland Development Program sought to reduce environmental degradation in upland areas by improving production by tenant farmers. The first step was to grant these farmers titles to the land. Initially reluctant to participate in the program for fear of reprisals from absentee landlords, a growing number of farmers felt reassured by program officials and joined in.

However, tensions between tenant farmers and landlords developed. On one occasion, an absentee landlord filed a claim against a former tenant. Even though the landlord had no legal title to the land, he decided to file a complaint for breach of contract over a sharecropping agreement. Under strong pressures, the farmer apologized and complied with the agreement. Unfortunately, this setback established a precedent. Here, the key issue was power. The landlord had the connections and influence to pressure one tenant farmer into complying with the alleged contractual agreement. Had the program organized tenant farmers to deal with this problem as a group, chances are they could have mobilized enough support to counterbalance the power of individual landlords (Poffenberger, 1990).

The intended beneficiaries of development are not a monolithic interest group.

Naturally, the intended beneficiaries of development are not a monolithic interest group. Because these populations often harbor a variety of interests and agendas, participation is likely to trigger conflict among them. If the proper checks and balances between the people and their leaders do not exist, participatory processes can be corrupted by special interest groups. In the Upland Development Project in the Philippines mentioned above, once activities got under way, project officials gave local people a free hand in the development of tenant organizations. Initially, a single organization was formed, but soon problems evolved. Although the project had assumed that tenant farmers shared similar economic and cultural characteristics and therefore had similar interests, it eventually became apparent that there were at least two distinct populations within the community: a large group of fourth-generation tenants and a small number of new migrants. The new migrants were better educated and also appeared to have stronger leadership skills, so they

were the first to be elected as officers in the organization. Soon they began to monopolize project resources and to favor kin and friends, sparking hostilities between long-term residents and new migrants. Program officials moved quickly, calling community meetings to create sectoral sub-organizations to plan and implement agroforestry activities. As more leadership positions opened up, the fourth-generation farmers found spots for their representatives (Poffenberger, 1990).

Something similar happened with the women in the community. Initially, grassroots organizations showed a distinct male bias. Project planners assumed that men were the appropriate representatives of households. Excluded from the project, women created their own group and forced the project organizers to reconsider their original assumptions. Eventually, women were incorporated into community organizations (Poffenberger, 1990).

Regarding the selection of leaders and women's participation, project managers prevented further conflict by bringing together organizations representing interest groups that had been left out of decision-making. They also recognized the need to intervene to modify project mechanisms, including those for distributing resources among a larger number of interest groups.

4. Ensuring a More Equitable Distribution of Benefits Locally

In assisting small communities in developing countries, development-cooperation agencies frequently work through the official leadership without knowing whether channels for participation and accountability exist. When these mechanisms are lacking, the benefits of external assistance are likely to be distributed selectively through patron-client networks supported by the leadership. In such cases, it is important that external agencies require leaders to set mechanisms in place to ensure the "transparency" of their decisions and actions.

This was the case in 1988, when the World Resources Institute began to help regional indige-

> *When these mechanisms for participation are lacking, the benefits of external assistance are likely to be distributed selectively through patron-client networks supported by the leadership.*

nous peoples' organizations in Ecuador develop and negotiate projects within the context of the Tropical Forest Action Plan. From 1988 to 1990, WRI together with COMUNIDEC and CIDESA (Fundación de Capacitación e Investigación para el Desarrollo Socio-Ambiental)—two in-country supporting NGOs—worked with grassroots organizations to draft project profiles for submission to international donors.

One project involved 12 fishing cooperatives from the Afro-Ecuadorean communities of the coastal mangrove forests of Ecuador's Esmeraldas province. These cooperatives were organized into a confederation, ACCEA (Asociación de Cooperativas del Cantón Eloy Alfaro), that received a small grant from an international donor and thus became an important broker for development assistance to the cooperatives. In 1990, donors renewed their interest in the federation's project profile, but requested specific action plans involving strong community participation. However, the confederation leadership had by then developed a strong sense of project ownership and was reluctant to follow COMUNIDEC and CIDESA's call for a participatory planning process involving each of the cooperatives. The leadership argued that it should be responsible for project planning and implementation because it knew what the cooperatives needed. In addition, the leaders complained that broad participation would further delay the process, that they

could not afford to take much time away from income-generating activities, and that coordinating and planning workshops would be difficult because cooperatives were spread out across a large, hard-to-traverse mangrove area and transportation was lacking.

When the time for elections came, the leaders of the confederation argued that a change of command would set the project back. By then it had become apparent that they had a weak following among the communities and that their support base rested on a network of "clients" that they had created by selectively distributing the financial resources under their control.

The leaders of the confederation insisted on keeping the planning process within their headquarters while COMUNIDEC and CIDESA remained adamant that decentralizing planning and implementation was essential. Because the two NGOs had direct access to potential donors and it was believed that they could block the flow of funds, the confederation finally agreed that each cooperative could carry out its own planning. Funds for the projects were then deposited directly in the bank accounts of each cooperative. As for the confederation leaders, their important role in organizing and conducting the workshops was recognized, and they also received a grant to purchase and operate a canoe with an outboard motor to facilitate transportation to workshops.

In this case, COMUNIDEC and CIDESA's firm stand on both participation and accountability avoided the uneven distribution of benefits and the further polarization of factions within and among the cooperatives, thereby strengthening the organization. As this case shows, NGOs and donors must always understand the impact that their support is likely to have on local organizations. Specifically, they must make sure that their efforts do not promote factionalism and inequity, but instead make organizations more capable and democratic.

III. Building Bridges: Reforming Policy-Making Institutions and Processes

Since governments ultimately decide how policy is made and implemented and who participates in public decision-making, their willingness to initiate a dialogue with many sectors of society is key to building new structures of governance. Some of the main changes that governments must initiate in environmental policy-making include the creation of agencies that can foster stakeholder participation when environmental problems and their solutions are defined.

If governments recognize their inability to address all public issues adequately, they will be more likely to create conditions under which citizen organizations can better address their own needs. On the other hand, if new structures of governance are to be effective, civil society must get organized to help accomplish the tasks that governments have neglected. NGOs, grassroots groups, and the business sector must move beyond criticizing governmental action or inaction and build their own capacities to propose viable options that address the problems they articulate. They must also learn how to better work together to generate independent information that can broaden the range of choices people can make as participatory democracies evolve.

This chapter provides some examples of the changes now taking place within both government and civil society that are leading to greater participation. In particular, it describes and illustrates the enhanced role of NGOs and other independent-sector institutions in information production and dissemination.

A. The Changing Role of Government Institutions

We are now witnessing the beginning of a move away from the interventionist state that was to meet all public needs. The growing expectation within civil society is that governments become more democratic and responsive to society's diverse concerns. During the 1980s, non-governmental organizations (NGOs), grassroots organizations (GROs), and new political parties in the developing world and in the former socialist bloc successfully pressured governments to make decisions more democratically and to pay more attention to environmental issues. These efforts coincided with those of a growing international NGO movement trying to reform development assistance and the lending practices of bilateral and multilateral donors, especially concerning projects affecting natural resources.

As a result, in Latin America for example, countries such as Mexico, Colombia, and Chile have passed new laws requiring governments to establish environmental planning committees with broad social representation at the provincial or local levels. Nations such as Argentina, Mexico, and Colombia have also set up or are considering creating high-level government offices to investigate citizens' environmental complaints and to prosecute as needed (EWLA, 1994; SEDESOL, 1993).

Meanwhile, a new generation of state agencies responsible for the environment has emerged in many developing countries. Many such agencies, which emerged during the late 1980s and early 1990s when government budgets and bureaucracies were scaled down, have planning and coordination capacities, but are not necessarily responsible for implementation. Few have the sizable financial resources that most sectoral ministries have. Some examples of these new bureaucratically and fiscally lean agencies in Latin America are the national environmental commissions (CONAMAs) in Chile and Guatemala and the secretariats of the environment in El Salvador and Honduras.

A lack of resources has forced some of these bodies to view consensus-building and participatory methods as important tools for policy formulation. Charged with coordinating environmental policy, they must gather support for their agendas from the more powerful sectoral ministries. Similarly, because these new agencies frequently draw on international funds or loans, they are more eager to incorporate representation mechanisms and participatory methods—often, a condition of funding.

In Bolivia, the General Secretariat of the Environment (SEGMA) was until recently the state agency in charge of environmental planning and coordination. Formed in 1990 with a tiny budget, it has since 1991 received most of its operating funds from international organizations (including multilateral banks, bilateral agencies, and private organizations). But SEGMA turned this apparent weakness into a strength by catalyzing and fostering greater participation in national environmental planning. For example, SEGMA worked closely with NGOs to develop the environmental report that Bolivia submitted to UNCED in 1992. Similarly, the Bolivian Environmental Action Plan (PAAB) that SEGMA prepared grew out of a thorough consultation process. At several regional and national workshops, representatives from various ministries and from civil society (workers, business people, ethnic groups, farmers, etc.) reviewed, discussed, and suggested amendments to PAAB's proposals (SEGMA, 1993).

The Chilean National Commission for the Environment (CONAMA) was developed to function as a *coordinating body* so that environmental

policy-making and implementation would not be concentrated in one agency or ministry with too few resources to meet formidable challenges. These include getting powerful ministries, the business community, NGOs, and the public to agree on the changes needed to improve environmental management and the speed at which these should occur. CONAMA now sets the direction for the agencies and ministries implementing environmental policies, though the sectoral bodies are still responsible for the impact of their activities on the environment.

CONAMA's political direction comes from a committee comprised of the Ministries of the Economy, Education, Public Works, Agriculture, Mining, Housing and Transport, among others. Each ministry's environmental unit is responsible for addressing environmental issues in its purview, according to the policies set forth by CONAMA. Regional environmental commissions known as the COREMAs have also been established, in accordance with Chile's commitment to decentralization. The COREMAs must develop environmental plans and programs to reflect regional needs and the overall environmental policy set by CONAMA.

CONAMA has also been responsible for drafting a new, comprehensive environmental law that makes provisions for citizen participation in CONAMA and the COREMAS. CONAMA's consultative council will include two representatives from the academic community, two from business, two from labor, and two from NGOs (WRI, 1994–1995; EWLA, 1994).

The structure of CONAMA illustrates a way by which governments can begin to address environmental problems intersectorally by drawing on the institutional resources of other ministries, by establishing mechanisms that allow representatives of various interest groups to review and comment on the agency's activities, and by setting up the mechanisms to enable the systematic participation of various stakeholders in planning and monitoring.

Given their small size and limited resources, new bodies like CONAMA and the secretariats for the environment will need to work closely with both local governments and various groups representing civil society, allowing them to play an increasingly important role in policy-making and implementation. A primary challenge is converting in-country or international pressures for broader participation into new opportunities for dialogue, thus enabling policy-makers to see reforms as an asset rather than as a threat to the governing process. *(See Box 2.)*

Box 2. CCAD: Coordinating Policies at the Regional Level

The Central American Commission for Environment and Development (CCAD) is another new-generation institution seeking to influence regional decision-makers by facilitating the exchange of information and by providing a forum in which different interest groups can address specific regional issues.

While the countries of Central America are ethnically and historically diverse, they face similar economic and social problems, among them slow economic growth, widespread poverty, and rapid population growth. At the same time, all are watching their natural resource base deteriorate through land degradation, the destruction of coastal resources, excessive pesticide use, and poor waste management. The size of the countries, their proximity, and the nature of their problems make regional coordination a logical response (Annis et al., 1992; Leonard, 1989).

With this general purpose in mind, the presidents of Central America created the CCAD in 1989. The Commission is composed of the heads of the ministries (or agencies) most directly responsible for environmental policy in each of the seven Central American countries. CCAD's principal mission is to promote policy coordination, develop new funding, build institutional capacities, make information available, and foster citizens' participation to help address the region's pressing environmental and development needs (CCAD, 1992).

CCAD's secretariat is an extremely lean operation. Its staff of five—the executive secretary (appointed by CCAD's members), two

assistants, an accountant, and a messenger—is supplemented by consultants who take on specific tasks. Initially, CCAD functioned mainly as a forum that all Central American Ministers dealing with the environment used to discuss issues of common concern. But by 1992 it was also involved in planning related to regional environmental and development issues. The Secretariat has become a reliable source of information on who is doing what in environment and development in Central America, and the Commission is building its capacities to gather, organize, and distribute information on these issues throughout the region and beyond.

CCAD brings together governments, NGOs, grassroots organizations, and international institutions to discuss and analyze problems and to develop policy recommendations and action plans with broad support. CCAD has designed a consultation methodology for elaborating action plans and international conventions across the region. Through multisectoral dialogues lasting 12 to 16 months, hundreds of individuals representing diverse interests (government, business, NGOs, grassroots) discuss and rank policy proposals that presidents and parliaments in the region then adopt *(see Chart)*. Examples include the Central American Agenda for Environment and Development (ACAAD), a joint regional statement on priority actions adopted in 1992 for addressing environment and development issues in the area, and the Central American Tropical Forest Action Plan (PAFTCA) sponsored by CCAD in 1991, which has drawn over US$160 million in support of better forest management in the

Box 2. continued

isthmus. With PAFTCA came the Regional Convention for the Management and Conservation of Natural Forest Ecosystems and the Development of Forest Plantations. Signed in 1993, this convention provides a framework for policy and institutional reform in the forestry sector, in accordance with the needs and interests expressed by user groups during consultations.

To pave the way for legal reforms across the region, CCAD helped create other regional bodies to bridge gaps between governments and civil organizations within nations. The Central American Inter-parliamentary Commission on the Environment (CICAAD), for instance, brings together representatives of the legislatures from the seven countries to push for international conventions and policy reforms in the national congresses. Acting on reports of toxic waste dumping in the region, CCAD and CICAAD joined forces to help set up regional networks of NGOs and government bodies to monitor attempts to dump waste in Central America. Late in 1992, the seven countries of the isthmus signed an agreement to ban the importation or international transport of a wide range of hazardous materials. Coupled with the networks' written information and public education campaigns on hazardous waste shipments, this ban is making it difficult for corrupt entrepreneurs and politicians to profit from illegal waste dumping in the region.

Throughout Central America, CCAD is helping strengthen national environmental agencies so they can increase public participation in decision-making. In 1994, it began a project to train the staff of government environmental agencies in Central America in participatory methods for policy formulation.

Similarly, the quest for regional integration has led to the "Alliance for Sustainable Development," adopted in October 1994 by the seven Central American presidents. Under CCAD leadership, the Alliance has emerged as a forum in which various interested parties discuss and identify priority actions. For example, in February 1995, CCAD and The World Conservation Union (IUCN) together carried out a planning workshop in Panama to identify priorities and collaborating organizations across the region to implement the forestry, biodiversity, and environmental law commitments made by Alliance signatories. One hundred representatives from governments, NGOs, the business sector, research institutions and grassroots organizations from the seven Central American countries attended. CCAD's access to the highest levels of policy-making and its participatory approach account for its success in getting NGOs, ministers, and presidents to endorse the initiatives and proposals it sponsors. The prestige that presidential support affords CCAD, its low profile, and the organization's commitment to democratic processes and to remaining small and agile also contribute.

B. The Role of the Independent Sector

Independent sector organizations are increasingly filling the vacuum left by shrinking governments. The so-called independent sector encompasses grassroots organizations (GROs) and non-governmental organizations (NGOs) ranging from universities and research institutions to community support groups. Its agendas and constituencies are quite heterogeneous. Independent-sector organizations are non-profit—unlike most consulting and other firms—and most NGOs guard their independence from political parties. But they are not apolitical. Along with the research, public information, or social services that they provide, many such groups try to influence political decisions and to promote their constituencies' perspectives and interests.

Most NGOs guard their independence from political parties. But they are not apolitical.

---

1. Relying on Self-Help: The Growth of GROs

Organizing for self-help on the grassroots level is scarcely a new phenomenon. Marginal populations have traditionally used self-help groups to meet local needs and to protect their interests from the advances of powerful external forces. In Latin America, indigenous communities have since colonial times managed to retain their land by holding collective titles. Often, locally elected governments pool labor to meet collective needs and organize ritual activities. In these communities, most interactions with outsiders take place through elected authorities (Aguirre Beltrán, 1962; Wolf, 1957).

Rural and urban groups who have been marginalized have formed grassroots organizations (GROs) to fight for specific rights and benefits for their members. Frequently, their mode of operation is self-help. Some GROs, such as co-ops, credit unions, and farmer's unions, operate within legal frameworks. Others, such as neighborhood groups or village committees, are informal and not legally constituted. Top decision-making positions in GROs are held by leaders elected by the rank and file, and leaders account fully to members. GROs rely heavily on in-kind and monetary contributions or fees from their members. Depending on their size and scope, they might hire professionals, who in most instances answer to the elected leaders. Many of these groups have organized expressly to manage the natural resources that afford them a living.

The experience of the Zapotec community forestry enterprises (CFEs) in Oaxaca, Mexico, illustrates how grassroots groups in rural areas have organized to manage their natural resources. During the early 1980s, these communities organized to stop the renewal of timber concessions on their lands by private and decentralized government agencies. Over the previous 25 years, the Zapotecs had watched such concessionaires strip the forest of its best wood, leaving little or no benefits to the nearby communities.

Still, in those years (1950–1980), the Pueblos Mancomunados, a communal enterprise, got to develop its own method of timber extraction. After confrontations with local lumber companies—clashes that were widely publicized by NGOs with the support of the mass media—several communities were granted concessions in 1982 to manage the forest through negotiations with regional and federal government officials (López and Gerez Fernández, 1993; Winder, 1992; Bray, 1991). Subsequently, they either expanded or set up new CFEs to extract and sell lumber collectively. In many cases now, the enterprises handle all timber activities, from elaborating a management plan, felling trees, and extracting lumber to operating the saw mills, making sales, and carrying out forest conservation activities.

Through these CFEs, communities have obtained the capital needed to manage the forest, bypass local intermediaries, and compete in the regional and national timber market. With the technical support of advisors from NGOs and the Forestry Subsecretariat of the Ministry of Agriculture and Hydraulic Resources (SARH), ten of these communities formed the Unión de Comunidades y Ejidos Forestales de Oaxaca (UCEFO) in 1986 to provide them with technical forest-management services. By 1992, its members were supplying 25 percent of the timber produced in Oaxaca.

UCEFO's experience shows how traditional organizational structures can be used to improve people's living conditions. Relying on their ancestral social institutions and the help of NGOs and the media, the Zapotecs of Oaxaca mobilized their communities in support of a regional movement. Once they obtained the forestry concessions, the Zapotecs extended their traditional self-governing mechanisms to the management of the CFEs, which helped keep their operations accountable to the communities.

2. Lending Support and Expertise: The New Role of NGOs

NGOs comprise a wide variety of service institutions that design and execute development or environment projects. Often, NGOs engage in dialogue with the government, hoping to influence public policies affecting the population that they serve. Private non-profit organizations that operate within a legal framework, they are staffed and led by paid professionals, para-professionals, or volunteers. In Latin America, NGOs are financially supported by such development-cooperation institutions as northern NGOs, private voluntary organizations (PVOs), private foundations, multilateral institutions, bilateral agencies, governments, and in-country philanthropies.

NGOs have lent critical support to marginal groups struggling for better lives. In countries such as Bolivia and Ecuador where government's outreach capacity is weak, NGOs have also provided basic services in the areas of health, agricultural extension, and credit. In short, NGOs have often helped articulate grassroots needs and found the technical and economic resources to meet them.

Like other political and economic brokers, NGOs have sometimes knitted patron-client relations with the communities they serve, setting themselves up as spokespersons, decision-makers, and exclusive channels of outside technical and financial assistance to marginal populations (Caroll, 1992; Bebbington et al. 1992a; Tendler, 1982). But, as the poor become better organized and develop the capacity to deliver such services, NGOs must cultivate new specialized skills or risk being redundant (Zazueta, 1993; Van Sant, 1987). This prospect should not trouble NGOs since it is quite consistent with their stated beliefs in grassroots autonomy and self-help (Bebbington et al., 1992).

In general, NGOs that have helped strengthen GROs enter into collaborative relationships based on comparative advantages and an effective division of labor. *(See Box 3.)* To fully assume a supportive role for GROs, NGOs must

1. build their own capacity to generate, analyze, and disseminate information;

2. develop their skills to properly assist GROs in project design, management, and fund raising; and

3. acquire the technical knowledge needed to advise GROs on development/environment activities (Zazueta, 1993).

C. Fostering Participation

An important challenge facing governments and independent sector organizations is how to draw on and strengthen the independent sector's emerging capacities to take part in the governing process. How participation will take place and the extent of its role in decision-making will vary by situation. Yet, four basic forms of participation have been identified: participation through consultation, monitoring and oversight in policy-making, community involvement in decision-making and implementation, and participation through information production and dissemination.

1. Participation Through Consultation

The key to fostering participation in the process leading to decision-making is policy dialogue. Consultation is one way to carry out policy dialogue. In it, government brings stakeholders into the discussion about options concerning the issues at hand, encouraging them to express their needs and views and to share their experiences. In this way, an array of options and possibilities will emerge. Consultation is relevant to both macro-economic decisions (national planning, and legal as well as institutional reforms) and local policy decisions (regional or municipal projects involving particular communities).

Box 3. A New Division of Labor

The collaboration between the Center for Social and Ecological Studies (CESE), a Mexican NGO, and the Organization Against the Contamination of Lake Patzcuaro (ORCA), a GRO, illustrates how the right division of labor between NGOs and GROs can benefit both.

Since 1983, CESE and ORCA have been working together to improve ORCA's capacity to develop technologies and policies that could reverse the destruction of Lake Patzcuaro. In the last ten years, ORCA has organized all 28 fishing communities on the lake; tested simple technologies to reduce erosion; worked with the communities to make sure that government programs will incorporate these and other technologies in local use; and established inter-community mechanisms to ensure local partici-

pation in the planning and implementation of government programs.

With long-term financial support from the Dutch Humanistic Institute for International Cooperation (HIVOS), CESE has helped ORCA become a strong regional organization noted for broad community participation. In the process, the three organizations developed a working relationship: periodically, they review objectives, accomplishments, and methods, learning from their experience and incorporating these lessons into future program activities. Currently, ORCA participates in a regional planning committee representing the interests of the fishing communities. In addition, the technologies developed by ORCA have now been adopted by other government programs (Zazueta, 1993; Esteva, 1994).

Consultation is particularly well-suited for situations in which the state has to make decisions that affect many groups. Often, such issues as the formulation of new laws or the construction of large public works, such as dams and roads are involved. Not a part of decision-making per se, consultation is a neutral mechanism for promoting broad policy dialogue among stakeholders—one that decision-makers can use to get a better understanding of the issues under consideration. Through consultations, governments increase stakeholders' opportunities to express their needs, concerns, and proposals.

Decisions rarely spring directly from consultations, which are not designed to delegate decision-making to stakeholders. From the stakeholder's standpoint, consultation processes are best seen as an opportunity for expression. From the standpoint of policy-makers, they present the chance to listen. Through consultation, policy-makers can also figure out who is likely to support or oppose an initiative and how to increase support.

Well managed consultations inform interested parties on the rationale behind plans and proposals under consideration. They can also help stakeholders develop a keener understanding of each other's needs, increase options for solving problems, and identify points or common interests around which actions can be taken virtually unopposed. *(See Box 4.)*

2. Monitoring and Oversight in Policy-making

Agencies with programmatic mandates have been able to involve stakeholders in policy-making by using task forces to formulate recommendations on issues or problems. But often task forces disappear once the ink on the recommendations is dry. Instead, they should be turned into standing committees with varied ongoing roles. For example, steering committees frequently play an important role in oversight and in establishing broad directions for specific initiatives, but have no responsibilities for how actions are carried out.

23

Box 4. Characteristics of Effective Consultation

The Central American Agenda for Environment and Development (ACAAD) identifies regional priority actions to advance environmentally sound development. ACAAD sprang from a broad, multi-purpose consultation conducted by CCAD. One aim was to heighten awareness of the region's major environmental problems and to build regional consensus around corrective actions. The second was to build the capacity and image of CCAD as a legitimate catalyst for policy dialogue in Central America, partly by strengthening relations between CCAD and other regional organizations, the National Environmental Commissions (CONAMAs), NGOs, grassroots groups, business guilds, etc.

The ACAAD consultation process, carried out from May 1991 to May 1992, consisted of three regional workshops and seven intersectoral national workshops. *(See Diagram 1.)* As the diagram shows, the consultation built consensus among stakeholders, fed sound information into the process at several stages, and strengthened policy-makers' commitment to the consultation process and its outputs.

Four key elements contributed to ACAAD's success:

1. A two-pronged inclusive approach. To build support for the agenda throughout the region, CCAD involved the United Nations Development Programme (UNDP) and the World Conservation Union (IUCN) in planning the consultation. Similarly, CCAD invited external governmental and non-governmental organizations (the Canadian and Finnish development agencies, UNDP, Conservation International and World Resources Institute) to provide technical and financial assistance. CCAD also asked each country's national commission for the environment to invite a broad range of NGO representatives to help organize and facilitate workshops in coordination with

the commission. Some 560 persons from 356 organizations attended, representing laborers, peasants, ethnic groups, women, and businesses. Various ministries and regional agencies, including those from provincial and municipal governments, were also represented (CCAD, 1992).

2. Integrity. CCAD carefully avoided any impression that the consultation was biased or was being manipulated by informing all participants that this was consultation, not decision-making. The NGOs that helped facilitate the meetings were given an important role in planning and implementing the process. With technical assistance from World Resources Institute, CCAD developed a standard workshop methodology. Facilitators were trained to use, and allowed to modify, this methodology during a regional workshop. They clearly understood the purposes of the consultation and the methodology to be followed, and had a sense of "owning" the process.

After the seven national workshops were carried out (one per country) and the outputs were tabulated, another regional workshop was held with the facilitators to review and ratify the results. Once the seven facilitators reached an agreement, CCAD staff met with advisors from the Ministries on the Commission to find the wording to insure that the seven governments would endorse results. No substantive alterations were made at this last stage.

3. Analysis on the basis of sound information. Sound information kept workshop discussions tightly focussed on the analysis of issues and feasible actions. For instance, the seven consultative workshops concentrated on eight priorities identified during the first regional workshop held in San José, Costa Rica in May 1991. These priority areas were then discussed during the seven intersectoral

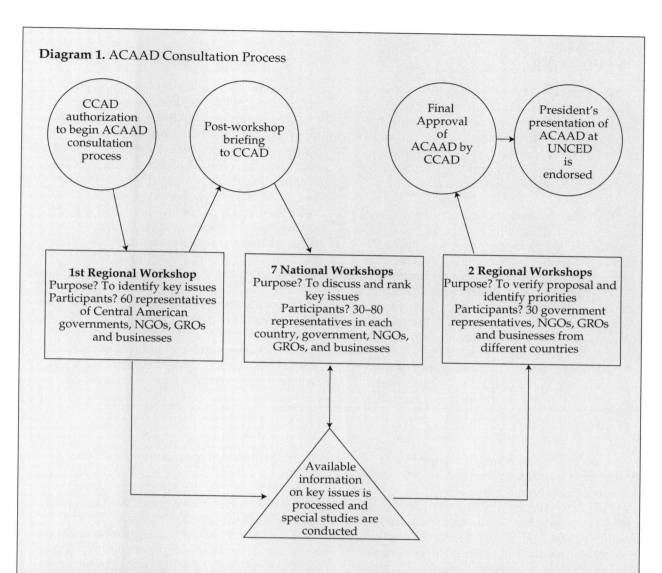

Diagram 1. ACAAD Consultation Process

CCAD authorization to begin ACAAD consultation process

Post-workshop briefing to CCAD

Final Approval of ACAAD by CCAD

President's presentation of ACAAD at UNCED is endorsed

1st Regional Workshop
Purpose? To identify key issues
Participants? 60 representatives of Central American governments, NGOs, GROs and businesses

7 National Workshops
Purpose? To discuss and rank key issues
Participants? 30–80 representatives in each country, government, NGOs, GROs, and businesses

2 Regional Workshops
Purpose? To verify proposal and identify priorities
Participants? 30 government representatives, NGOs, GROs and businesses from different countries

Available information on key issues is processed and special studies are conducted

national workshops by representatives from diverse social groups. Current information on the selected issues and proposed actions presented as each workshop opened helped participants frame the discussion in smaller groups and assess problems and actions realistically. It also provided a common point of reference for all participants and permitted them to assess each other's interventions.

4. Political support and follow-up. Key to the success of this consultation process was the fact that CCAD's executive secretary had the mandate and access needed to get the process politically endorsed. Initially, some members of CCAD were apprehensive about the participatory nature of the consultation. But the group's executive secretary regularly gave the ministry members of CCAD brief progress reports on the consultations, and the ministers joined in by inaugurating the national intersectoral workshops. As the consultation moved along, the CCAD ministers grew more comfortable, and they fully endorsed the process and the recommendations once the agenda was published.

Box 4. continued

Timing was just as important. The endorsement of the agenda by the Central American presidents, and its wide distribution both within the region and internationally one month before UNCED in 1992, made it a powerful statement on the region's challenges and priorities related to environment and development.

Once the finished agenda was disseminated among participants and others, CCAD developed a strategic plan for implementing it. Follow-up activities have included the development of the Central American Environmental Fund (to finance initiatives by governments, NGOs, grassroots groups, and the private sector) and the design of a program to strengthen the capacities of the national environmental agencies of the seven Central American countries to formulate and promote policies incorporating the views of all interested parties.

Before the Central American Agenda for Environment and Development was devised, CCAD was not widely known among environment and development groups in Central America. But the consultation process helped establish it as a service organization capable of drawing people together to discuss important issues and to reach agreements on action. What's more, CCAD has no implementation capacity or any intention to develop it. Other national and regional sectoral agencies and organizations thus perceive it mainly as a resource and not as a competitor.

The process leading to the Central American Agenda for Environment and Development exemplifies how consultation can foster consensus for action around important issues while helping cultivate an informed public and building the sponsoring agency's credibility.

In most cases, committees are legitimating mechanisms intended to increase support and reduce opposition among stakeholders, as well as to ensure that wide-ranging information and perspectives get incorporated into decision-making and implementation. Since committees typified by broad representation can help make sure that policies, projects, or activities do not fall hostage to the interests of the few, the selection of committee members is extremely important.

The National Environmental Fund in Bolivia (FONAMA) illustrates various ways in which representatives from the public might take part in monitoring and oversight of governmental policy-making. FONAMA was created in 1990 as a decentralized public agency directly accountable to the President of Bolivia. Created to attract and administer funds in support of investments and projects to protect Bolivia's environment and natural resources, FONAMA had by October 1992 signed donation agreements with interna-

tional cooperation organizations for over US$50 million.

Several factors undergird FONAMA's fund-raising success, but two stand out. One is that FONAMA had the political support of Bolivia's president. The other is that the Fund included NGO representatives in decision-making positions at various levels of operation. For example, FONAMA's charter specifies that LIDEMA, a prestigious league of Bolivian environmental organizations, is one of five voting members of FONAMA's board of directors, its highest decision-making body.

Since 1984, LIDEMA has played an increasingly important role advocating environmentally sound development in Bolivia. Besides voting privileges, LIDEMA's participation on FONAMA's board of directors gives it access to information and the authority to monitor FONAMA's activities. Because LIDEMA's responsibilities and loyalties are with its members and not the government, its participation on FONAMA's board of directors is one of "an independent watchdog." Indeed, LIDEMA has blown the whistle on several occasions when it has felt that government officials have not followed agreed-upon procedures.

FONAMA, whose accounts are managed through agreements established with donors has engaged other NGOs, universities, and grassroots organizations in its funding activities too. For instance, the agreement with the United States concerning the account of the Enterprise for the Americas Initiative (EAI) stipulates that funds are to be used to finance NGOs, grassroots groups, and research institutions and that funding-allocation decisions are to be made by an administrative committee composed of eight people, four from the government and the other four from the independent sector.

To make sure that the interests of these diverse groups would be properly represented in the administrative committee, FONAMA held a workshop to inform groups of the purpose of the fund and the terms of the grants, and to elect four candidates—to be confirmed by the government—and their substitutes to form part of the administrative committee. During the same workshop, a follow-up plan to ensure accountability was developed, along with communication-and-feedback mechanisms for the organizations and the elected committee members (FONAMA, 1992). To lend more credibility to the EAI and cultivate relations with NGOs, GROs, and research institutions, FONAMA hired for the job of administrator of the account someone who knows the NGO landscape in Bolivia and who is well known and widely respected by independent groups, government officials, and international donors.

Steering and administrative committees can help ensure ongoing participation in decision-making. But they will only work if government officials are truly committed to openness. Ideally, as the case of FONAMA shows, government officials should leave it to the stakeholders themselves to select the individuals or organizations that they believe will truly represent their views and interests.

3. The Involvement of Civil Society in Decision-making and Implementation

Some governments seeking to reform institutions and the way they make decisions have gone one step further and delegated the planning and implementation of a program to organizations from the independent sector. In such cases, citizens' groups actually define problems, formulate solutions and action plans, and help implement activities. This form of participation is appropriate mostly at the local level or for programs or projects affecting a small community.

Increasingly, governments are turning over the management of protected natural areas to NGOs and grassroots groups. In South America, a case in point is the national park Isiboro Secúre in the Department of El Beni in Bolivia. Most of the parklands are located within a territory traditionally occupied by Indian communities. In 1992, following negotiations between Indian organizations and the government, the latter decided to delegate park administration to the community organization. And despite problems with a few pending claims of ownership by private farmers over some of the lands now incorporated into the protected area, the local Indian organization continues to administer the park successfully.

In other countries, such as Mexico, Guatemala, Honduras, Belize and Costa Rica, the government has also turned to NGOs to help manage national parks and other protected areas. The Calakmul Bioreserve in Mexico's southeastern state of Campeche is one example of such NGO participation. In 1992, Calakmul's management was turned over to a consortium of state government officials, community groups, and NGOs. In Guatemala, the NGO Defensores de la Naturaleza lobbied Congress in 1990 to issue a legislative decree creating the Sierra de las Minas Biosphere Reserve. Subsequently, the National Council for Protected Areas (CONAP)—a government agency—invited Defensores de la Naturaleza to help manage the newly created reserve. CONAP has also supported the NGO's efforts to purchase additional lands to protect. Similarly, in Guatemala the Centro de Estudios para la Conservación, a research center within the University of San Carlos, currently administers the Biotopo El Quetzal, located in the central highlands.

Similar partnerships have evolved in Honduras, where in 1992 the government assigned the administration of the Refugio de Vida Silvestre Cuero Salado to Fundación Cuero Salado, an NGO created to raise awareness of the importance of protecting the park's wildlife. Late in 1992, CHODEFOR—the government forestry agency—signed an agreement with the NGO Aldea Global to administer the Cerro Azul park. CHODEFOR is currently negotiating with Fundación Fasquelle over the management of Cusuco National Park.

Often, community organizations and NGOs get involved in the management of protected areas because these organizations have heavily lobbied governments to create them. Also, states facing fiscal and technical constraints realize that international donors are more willing to provide funds for protected areas directly to NGOs than to government agencies. In addition, governments have found it difficult to implement effective controls in vast or remote protected areas where there is little or no state presence to begin with.

A higher level of participation is seen when the state delegates planning and implementation of a program to independent sector organizations. This is currently taking place in the Mexican Program for the Protection of the Tropical Forests (PROAFT). *(See Box 5.)*

Examples like PROAFT, where the government assigns an important planning function to inde-

---

Box 5. Delegating Planning: The Case of PROAFT in Mexico

PROAFT was born out of the recognition by Mexican officials in the Ministry of Agriculture and Hydraulic Resources (SARH) that the Mexican Tropical Forest Action Plan (TFAP) was failing to address key policy issues, such as intersectoral policy linkages and the needs of forest dwellers, thus contributing to the impoverishment of marginal populations, rapid deforestation, and biodiversity loss in the Mexican tropics. Furthermore, the documents of the plan, which had been elaborated with little consultation with local populations, were strongly biased toward the forestry sector.

To address these concerns within the Ministry, in mid-1992 the Undersecretary of Forestry invited some of the strongest critics of the government's forestry policy to review the TFAP and to propose an alternative course of action. As a result, the vertically conceived Mexican TFAP turned into PROAFT, a highly participatory process that combines planning with action and consultations with stakeholders. At a time when the side agreements for the North American Free Trade Agreement were under negotiation, tropical forest conservation became an important concern for former President Salinas. Indeed, he personally conferred decision-making authority to PROAFT's new leaders.

Over the next three years, a team of five people from two established NGOs (Gestión de Ecosistemas, AC, and Grupo de Estudios Ambientales, AC) and the National University (UNAM) was assembled to carry out PROAFT. A new NGO—PROAFT, AC—was formed to act as a counterpart and procure funds for the new three-pronged initiative. The first component of the project was a series of 16 tropical forestry studies. Some were generic, such as those on the expansion of cattle herding and legislation on resource use in the tropics while others were specific, such as performance evaluations of specific commissions or programs. These studies, carried out mainly on contract by NGOs and academics, organized the available information on the various

pendent sector organizations, are rare and face many obstacles. Nonetheless, when approached as an opportunity to identify action priorities supported by various stakeholders, it can result in a win-win situation for all parties concerned.

4. Information Production and Dissemination

Participation in policy dialogue also takes place through information production and dissemination. After all, policy dialogue is about *power.* Dialogue allows different interest groups or stakeholders with varying degrees of power to compete to make government policy responsive to their interests. Access to information on germane issues are crucial for all parties involved, especially in publicly debated matters. To level

Participation in policy dialogue also takes place through information production and dissemination. After all, policy dialogue is about power.

the playing field, governments must open up access to accurate and useful information to all involved. Similarly, citizens' groups should gather and disseminate information that helps both stakeholders and decision-makers fully understand the issues at stake.

---

topics, provided "a quick read" of the condition of natural resources, summarized the outcomes of government programs in tropical areas, and contained recommendations for improving those programs or initiating new activities or policies.

The second component was a series of Tripartite Alliances, through which PROAFT would promote grassroots initiatives to improve forest management by financing and providing technical assistance to 28 projects identified by the communities. NGOs and universities were invited to provide technical assistance to these community groups—thus the name Tripartite Alliances (SARH, the community, and an NGO or university).

The third component was a process of consultation consisting of four workshops carried out in various regions of the country. PROAFT presented priorities that were debated and amended in open discussions by representatives of NGOs, grassroots groups, business, and government officials from other ministries

and state governments. On average, 60 people attended each workshop.

Through this highly inductive and participatory process, PROAFT had by the fall of 1994 produced a new Mexican TFAP that harnessed knowledge and many viewpoints on problem definition. It also identified six priority lines of action. Each line of action included a series of proposed activities, and organizations that could carry them out were identified throughout the country.

Mexico's political and economic crisis in late 1994 and early 1995 has placed many government initiatives on hold, PROAFT among them. Nonetheless, PROAFT's highly participatory approach has led the new administration to review and approve the proposal. Because PROAFT is not only technically sound, but also incorporates the views of the various stakeholders, it appealed greatly to new government officials seeking to respond to the democratization of Mexican political institutions.

Ease of access to information is not only a matter of the extent to which key information is made publicly available, but also of its form. As often presented, potentially useful information is too technical or difficult to grasp. Indeed, without the following characteristics it is virtually useless:

1. It must be clear. Complex project rationales or formulations often go unchallenged, but that does not mean that they are convincing and solid. To be convincing, arguments for or against policies and projects must be understood by stakeholders. Technical studies are needed, even if they are sophisticated, but findings must be presented clearly and simply. Easy-to-understand statistics, percentages, indexes, case studies, illustrative examples, and testimonials from respected sources can all influence policy-making.

In recent years, rapid advances in geographical information systems (GIS) have made it possible to present complex data in ways that non-experts can easily understand. In Zambia, for instance, the Administrative Management Design Program (AMADE) is returning control over natural resources to local populations, who in the past were banned from game areas. AMADE has made extensive use of GIS not only to collect data but also to assess the environmental damage inflicted by poachers and others on game zones. The program has graphically shown local people how poaching, overgrazing, and the burning of vegetation can degrade a resource base that would otherwise help sustain them. Key in this process has been the training of local groups in administrative systems and in the use of geographical information systems that are easy to understand and operate (Pryjomko, 1993).

2. It must be objective and widely available. Sound decisions stem from objective information, and the public has the right to be informed on the various aspects of development programs and projects so it can assess for itself potential benefits and negative impacts. Information controlled by a few interested parties is likely to be used for their exclusive benefit. Furthermore, those who may be negatively affected by certain policies and programs will never get the chance to point out those programs' weaknesses, much less measures for mitigating them.

When in 1982 the Costa Rican government reintroduced the old idea of building a transoceanic pipeline to attract foreign investment and strengthen the nation's economy, the mass media were quick to praise the new opportunity. This time, environmental considerations that in the past had hampered the project were downplayed, and everyone emphasized the immense riches that the pipeline would bring to Costa Rica. However, the few dissenting voices opposing the project were convinced that the pipeline was not a sound proposal on either environmental or economic grounds.

By publicizing the weaknesses of the bidders' proposals and by showing how the calculations of potential benefits were grossly overblown, environmentalists enabled both decision-makers (the Costa Rican Congress) and the general public to reject the pipeline as a pipe dream rather than specifically as an environmental threat. Once the Costa Ricans were aware of the project's economic flaws, they were also keen on hearing about the dangers of pollution, deforestation, and oil spills.

3. It must be factual and sound. If information is to influence perception and understanding, it must contain the facts that directly support conclusions. Sweeping judgments and generalizations only polarize a dialogue (Forester, 1980).

Commitment to factual information proved vital to the successful outcome of an exercise in Participatory Rural Appraisal (PRA) conducted in Esmeraldas, Ecuador. PRA is a methodology that seeks to combine traditional and technical knowledge in problem identification and project planning. During the PRA, the black population of Esmeraldas revealed that a major problem for them was the encroachment of *mestizo* settlers into their traditional lands. The team conducting the PRA included several black leaders, who initially defined this problem as one of state discrimination against their communities. Whether or not there is a negative predisposition by many government officials in Quito toward the black population of Esmeraldas, black leaders could not substantiate the precise connections between official feelings toward blacks and the growing *mestizo* settlements in the region.

Articulating the problem from a racial perspective allowed local people to express their frustration with state officials, but elicited no proposals from Quito for solving the problem. So, digging deeper, the team identified the key contributing factor to the encroachment of *mestizos* onto lands formerly held by blacks—namely, the inability to rely on the judicial system to evict the settlers because few blacks hold congress-confirmed titles to the lands. Defining the problem in these terms immediately pointed to the specific action that could give Esmeraldas' blacks access to the national judicial system when *mestizo* settlers encroached—the ratification of communal land titles by the Congress.

4. It must incorporate the views of all involved parties. Gathering the factually based views of all parties concerned and of neutral knowledgeable sources will help produce information that both stakeholders and the general public consider reliable. This approach makes decisions based on such information more acceptable too and helps ensure that all the relevant impacts of every development action are properly weighted—important to both potential losers and winners.

For instance, those who stand to benefit from an agricultural or irrigation project might highlight the number of new jobs and the amount of foreign currency that export crops might bring. On the other hand, populations down river or environmental groups might stress the potential damage to ecosystems and populations from agrochemicals, water diversions, and agricultural chemical runoff. This is the case of the Mexican port of Mazatlán, in the state of Sinaloa, where both fishing and tourist activities are hurt by the runoff from nearby agricultural areas. Although municipal environmental officials have acknowledged the damage, they are up against powerful agricultural producers and the agrochemical industry. Including various viewpoints on data compilation, analysis, and review gives stakeholders the chance to raise questions and identify information gaps before decisions are made.

Of course, disagreements among stakeholders over factual information are inevitable. But the right questions will prompt all interested parties to gather the evidence needed to examine the issue more fully. For this reason, stakeholders must focus on specific issues and agree on which questions require additional information to answer.

Universities, policy research institutes, and NGOs are not perceived as deriving direct economic or political gain from the information they provide or the causes they advocate.

D. The Independent Sector as an Information Source

Universities, policy research institutes, and NGOs can influence policy-making significantly because, as independent sources of information, they are not perceived as deriving direct economic or political gain from the information they provide or the causes they advocate. But producing accurate information and analyses is not enough. To be effective, these organizations must present feasible policy options and build public opinion and constituencies around their concerns. NGOs must also in timely fashion get this information to those who know how to communicate and disseminate it. Here, the mass media play a key role: not only can they reach large numbers of people at once, but they can also clearly shape the outcome of policy dialogue and exert pressure around policy-making. For this reason, NGOs need strong links with both research organizations and the media. *(See Box 6.)*

Box 6. Information as Power

The ratification of Mexico's new forestry law illustrates how an alliance between a recently established forestry network, NGOs, and academics can influence a legislative process by obtaining and using sound information effectively. In November 1991, the Salinas administration rushed a major change in the agrarian reform law through Congress with little consultation or opportunity for input by citizens groups. At the center of this reform was the privatization of the *ejido*, Mexico's collective land-holding system. Despite many calls for a public debate by various political parties, as well as regional and national peasant organizations, President Salinas' initiative was passed and approved by Congress within one month with virtually no amendments. But such railroading had a high political cost, sparking friction within the country's official Institutional Revolutionary Party (PRI) and with peasant organizations throughout the country (Cuadernos Agrarios, 1992; Moguel et al., 1992).

Subsequently, in June 1992, Salinas tried to rush another bill through Congress. He was now proposing a complete revision of the 1986 Forestry Law, hoping to facilitate private sector investment in the forestry sector. This time around, things were not so easy. Opposition parties, congressmen from PRI, and peasant organizations were leery of the rapid pace of the reforms. Moreover, several major safeguards were omitted from the proposed text of the law, and no mention was made of the role and rights of forest dwellers (Indian communities and *ejidos*), the state's role in the growing free-market economy was not clearly stated, and natural resource conservation issues were dealt with only superficially (Chapela, 1992).

Seizing this opportunity, a loose network of NGOs and academics that had cooperated over several years with various Indian communities and forestry *ejidos* and had often collaborated with the little known and politically weak National Network of Forestry Organizations (Red NOCAF), moved quickly to point out the omissions in the text and to present solutions to the problems they raised. Red NOCAF and its newly found allies formed an informal network, that though relatively unknown in the public arena, had two resources at its disposal. One was information. After a decade of work with peasant lumber groups, the network understood both the problems in the forestry sector and the accomplishments and limitations of social forestry organizations. The second resource was extensive contacts with regional community forestry organizations across the nation. (During the 1980s, some members of the expanded network had supported a process to form a politically independent forestry network of peasant organizations.)

The network's approach to influencing the new forestry law was two-pronged. On the one hand, it sought to persuade Congress and the public to review the new legal initiative in light of its potential impact on social forestry in Mexico, and not just in light of government-sponsored free-market policies for the sector. On the other hand, the group sought to develop consensus and spark action among peasant lumber organizations on proposals to address issues neglected in the administration's initiative.

Using their government contacts, the members of the expanded network obtained a copy of the heretofore narrowly circulated draft of the administration's initiative before it was sent to Congress in March 1992. To provide an alternative perspective to the administration's free-market approach, the group gathered information on the dynamics of the forestry sector in various regions of the country and highlighted the accomplishments of regional peasant organizations. Shortly after President Salinas formally submitted the new law to Congress, the network made its findings public in a special issue of *El Cotidiano* (1992) (a magazine with many subscribers in Mexico City), held press conferences, and testified on the topic before the Mexican Congress. The main question this group raised before Congress was why, since Mexico had several successes in social forestry, the government had suddenly proposed a new development path that basically ignored a decade's worth of accomplishments.

The network provided enough information to tip the balance. Congress did not ratify the law immediately, and it requested more information—an unusual occurrence in Mexico's one-party political system. In addition, some of the network's individual members quickly staged forums with community forestry groups across the country to discuss the new forestry law, explore its implications, and develop consensus on amendments to the text. Meanwhile, they kept the issue before the public by testifying before Congress, writing newspaper articles, and appearing at press conferences. The information campaign lasted from early July to November 1992, when Congress finally passed the final version of the law.

The approved version incorporated several important proposals presented by the network. First, at several points throughout the text of the law, the *ejidatarios* and the Indian communities were mentioned as important users of the forest. Second, the notion of regional consultation committees was introduced as an example of how peasant organizations, timber industrialists, NGOs, and other stakeholders could have a say in which regulations were issued and how they were modified. The original initiative had considered only the formation of a national committee, which would favor private sector industrialists headquartered in Mexico City at the expense of regional community forestry organizations without the time or money to attend meetings there. Third, several forms of state control over exploitation of natural resources—among them, forestry permits and documentation to transport lumber—were reintroduced into the bill to deter the over-exploitation of natural resources. Similarly, the proposed law's leeway for concessions for the economic exploitation of protected areas and the unrestricted use of resources was reduced in the final version, which acknowledges the possibility of using resources in protected areas but makes all such concessions subject to the conditions stipulated in the Law of Protected Areas.

Red NOCAF received an additional benefit: as the national organizational platform in this process, the forums it held around the country, and the consequent media exposure contributed to recognition by regional organizations of the value of a national organization.

This case clearly demonstrates that even in a country like Mexico, where policy-making tends to be centralized, opportunities exist to influence decision-making. In the final analysis, it was the information produced by a group with no particular economic or political stake in the forestry sector in alliance with Red NOCAF that prompted regional peasant organizations to voice their concerns and legislators to change the administration's proposal.

A few examples of organizations with a strong focus on information production and dissemination are the Quantos Institute in Peru, which gathers and publishes information on economic, social, and environmental issues; CIPMA (Center for Environmental Research and Planning) in Chile, which publishes several newsletters aimed at lawmakers and municipal governments; and the Environmental Studies Group (GEA, AC) and the Center for the Promotion of Popular Development (CPDP) in Mexico, both of which produce environmental education materials on such topics as waste management, pesticide use, and agroecology erosion control. In Bogotá, Colombia, the news agency Prensa Verde (Green Press) is devoted exclusively to producing information on environmental issues. This agency gave *Semana*, the nation's most influential weekly magazine, facts and data that led it to conduct a thorough investigation of wildlife smuggling in Colombia. Many other NGOs in Colombia, such as FUNDEPUBLICOS, the Colegio Verde de Villa de Leiva, and Fundación Alma, periodically publish documents or newspaper inserts on environmental policy matters, the defense of the public interest, and the right of citizens to easy access to information.

Since many of today's environmental challenges are global, mechanisms and channels for exchanging information throughout the world must be strengthened. To close the still significant gap between Northern and Southern access to information and technology, cooperation between Northern and Southern organizations and institutions is essential.

Few Southern NGOs—or even universities and research centers—possess all the environmental and socioeconomic data needed to act upon government project and policy proposals. In particular, development NGOs cannot afford to divert their attention from grassroots action to the research and factual analysis needed to influence policy-making. Conversely, many Northern organizations—with almost limitless access to electronic databases—specialize precisely in processing and disseminating statistical and factual information but lack the knowledge of local views and policy context that their Southern peers possess. If NGOs and other organizations of civil society want to be more effective in the policy field, both North and South, they have to collaborate more on information exchange and dissemination.

An example of such cooperation is the Bank Information Center (BIC). This independent Washington-based NGO serves as a liaison for Southern NGOs and facilitates the flow of information among organizations concerned with the environmental impacts of projects financed with loans from multilateral development banks (MDB), including the World Bank, the Inter-American Development Bank, and the Asian Development Bank. BIC was formed in 1987 and has since established a worldwide information network. The information center typically waits for a request from Southern NGOs before investigating a project. If the information collected shows that the appropriate environmental impact assessment has not been conducted, or that the studies carried out warn against implementing a particular project, BIC lobbies the trustees of the MDBs, Capitol Hill, or other U.S. agencies involved with U.S. contributions to MDBs to change course.

BIC also provides information about World Bank activities to NGOs and other interested individuals. While BIC is clearly the MDBs' watchdog, over time it has earned these lenders' respect. Some MDB officials have grown to appreciate BIC's role and often cooperate with the group's information inquiries. More specifically, BIC has helped organize consultations between the international NGO community and the World Bank on developing and evaluating the World Bank's environmental policies. In 1994, for instance, BIC helped the World Bank convene a highly successful NGO consultation on implementing the Bank's 1991 forest policy.

IV. Building Ladders: Strengthening Grassroots' Capacity to Contribute to Policy-making

Policy dialogue will not take place unless governments are willing to listen and to develop ways of incorporating various interest groups into decision-making and unless these groups are equally willing and able to organize themselves and negotiate. Because large segments of the population have often been excluded from these processes, the democratization of policy-making requires strengthening people's organizations so that they can articulate their needs and negotiate skillfully. These groups should be able to define their own needs, propose specific activities, and carry out actions.

The democratization of policy-making requires strengthening citizens' organizations so that they can articulate their needs and negotiate skillfully.

A. Moving From Confrontation to Collaboration

In Latin America, governments and citizens groups are gradually leaving behind the confrontational approaches of the 1970s for more collaborative ways to address problems. In the region, governments have often played a key role in organizing grassroots groups. But these attempts, like those involving organized political parties, frequently become mechanisms for political control. Promises of payoffs in exchange for votes, or formation of patron-client relations between political bosses and local leaders, frequently result in the co-optation of local movements. The *ejido* system in Mexico during the mid-1930s, the syndicates in Bolivia during the 1950s, and the cooperative movements in Ecuador and Peru during the 1960s all exemplify state-driven efforts to organize—and co-opt—the peasantry. Later, as shanty towns grew in urban areas, political patrons developed links with neighborhood and squatter groups. Through these client-patron relations, marginal people sought titles to their urban land, potable water and sanitation, and other services in exchange for votes.

By the 1970s, the formal economy had failed to absorb the increasing numbers of migrants who had moved to the cities searching for jobs after the state abandoned rural development in favor of ill-conceived industrialization and large-scale cash crops for export (Farington and Bebbington, 1993). This failure contributed to the growth and radicalization of independent organizations that stepped up demands for social services and public works in the cities and for tenure rights in the countryside.

In the 1980s, the debt crisis and subsequent programs of structural adjustment led governments in the developing world to cut social spending and to re-formulate their role as central service providers. At the same time, non-governmental organizations working in grassroots development were brought in to help alleviate poverty, especially through programs designed to make structural adjustment less painful. These organizations were encouraged to scale-up their operations and take on ever larger responsibilities in service delivery, which until then had been in the hands of the state.

For instance, the Bolivian Institute of Agricultural Technology (IBTA), a government agency, has proposed that NGOs collaborate with community groups in handling agricultural extension in the highlands (Bebbington, 1991). Mexico's government has granted peasant unions with qualified staff the right to manage forests for timber extraction—a function that until recently was granted to only a few firms regulated by the Ministry of Agriculture (Bray et al., 1993; López and Gérez Fernández, 1993). In Honduras, El Salvador, and Nicaragua, NGOs and GROs are providing approximately 15 percent of the region's farmers with technical assistance on sustainable agricultural practices, surpassing the state's outreach capacity (Kaimowitz, 1993).

These trends, reinforced by pressures toward democratization, have helped forge new ways for government organizations and citizens groups to interact. Gradually, non-governmental and grassroots organizations are moving from a demand-oriented, confrontational approach to a more pragmatic one driven by concrete proposals that ultimately deliver more tangible benefits for their constituents or members.

In Mexico, for example, the early 1970s saw intense and sometimes violent agrarian conflicts resulting in the redistribution of prime agricultural land, particularly in the country's Northwest. During the late 1970s, the state tried to integrate producer organizations vertically. Groups that had obtained access to the land early in that decade proved more responsive to state policies of agroindustrial promotion. In some instances, these new organizations were able to work with older and more traditional private farmer associations that they had fiercely opposed a few years

earlier. The tactic paid off. By the early 1980s, many groups had established impressive agroindustrial complexes with state support (Fox and Gordillo, 1991; Zazueta, 1984).

Twenty years ago, few Indian communities in Ecuador had titles to their lands. During the 1960s and 1970s, as land colonization and petroleum prospecting advanced in the Amazon forest, many of these communities were driven from their ancestral lands. But by the 1980s, Indian federations and confederations mobilized to legalize ownership of those lands under the country's communal titling laws. Combining pressure, negotiation, alliances with other popular sectors, and massive marches into the capital city, these communities have claimed some important victories. In 1990, the government expanded the Huarani Indian Reserve by nearly two million acres. Later in 1992, a march of 10,000 people to Quito led by the Organization of Indigenous People of Pastaza (OPIP) resulted in the award of land titles totaling 2.75 million acres (40 percent of the province of Pastaza) to 19 communities (Bebbington et al., 1992).

Pressure tactics have worked. As Indian leaders themselves are ready to acknowledge, government efforts in favor of tenure rights and bilingual education have been strengthened significantly. Now, some believe that a shift to a more collaborative relation with government is needed to raise constituent's living standards (through, say, better health care systems, higher income, etc.). Without these amenities, many leaders also believe, their membership will flee (Bebbington et al., 1992). Overall, the main challenge facing these organizations is to earn government's support through a working relationship. To avoid being co-opted into endorsing political agendas that do not necessarily represent their interests, GROs and NGOs are developing proposals that both reflect their constituencies' needs and correspond to current policies. By putting their social and economic agendas within the context of state economic goals that favor their own interests (such as higher crop productivity, increased exports, improvement of marketing systems, and better management of natural resources), these organizations have remained fairly politically autonomous, even when the state endorses their work (Bebbington et al., 1992; Fox, 1992; Moguel et al., 1992; Bartra et al., 1991; Fox and Hernández, 1989).

If decision-making is to be opened up, GROs and NGOs must have greater input in policy-making and project design, and not just in implementation.

If decision-making is to be opened up, GROs and NGOs must have greater input in policy-making and project design, and not just in implementation. Similarly, resources must be channeled directly through these organizations. Governments cannot hold them accountable for service delivery under the guise of democratization when neither sufficient resources nor the necessary training to manage them are being made available to give these organizations a fair chance of success. In the collaborative relationship required, all parties concerned can gradually learn about each other's needs, abilities, and limitations. To take advantage of each other's structural strengths and minimize weaknesses, such partnerships require agreed-upon goals and means, good channels of communication, flexibility, and inventiveness (Zazueta, 1993).

Such mutually beneficial relationships between government agencies and grassroots organizations are rare. As previously mentioned, relationships between governments and marginal populations are clientelistic—that is, governments typically provide specific benefits in exchange for political favors. And while this kind of relationship has often given the poor some access to resources and services, it has been well documented that in the long run subordination tends to co-opt group leadership and undermine its autonomy, as well as its effectiveness in meeting constituent's needs (Fox, 1992).

To break this pattern, a facilitator—whether an organization, group, or individual—can identify opportunities for collaboration by matching government initiatives with the interests of marginal groups. Such match-making requires the ability to operate within the government and among marginal populations. If perceived as disinterested, the facilitator will have the legitimacy needed to communicate and to help interested parties develop common goals and activities for realizing them.

National NGOs, international NGOs, or a combination of both often make good facilitators. They understand how governments work, and many have well-established relations with the grassroots. International NGOs can be particularly helpful when governments feel the need to respond to international pressures. *(See Box 7.)*

B. Dispelling Two Myths About Marginal Populations

The use of terms such as "the poor," "the grassroots," or "marginal populations" evokes images of an economically deprived and politically disenfranchised mass. But working effectively with these groups means overcoming this initial stereotype and exploring further both the conditions that make diverse interests and identities emerge in seemingly homogeneous populations and the power relations among subgroups.

1. The poor are not a homogeneous interest group. In the rural societies of Andean Ecuador, Peru, and Bolivia, for example, organization beyond the community is hard to accomplish. Even though people in this region often have very similar needs and would benefit from cooperation, they take pride in their differences—whether in the clothes they wear or the patron saints they worship. Territorial disputes and competition for land often lie at the root of this emphasis on differences and can lead to factionalism, conflict, and even to violent confrontations among neighboring communities.

37

Box 7. Seizing the Opportunity

The Forestry Action Plan-Maya (PAF-Maya) in Guatemala illustrates how the convergence of interests among a government agency, a GRO, and an international NGO can lead to a far-reaching collaboration that promotes policy dialogue. PAF-Maya came about as a result of the criticisms that the worldwide Tropical Forest Action Plan (TFAP) initiative received. Several assessments had established that the TFAP had failed to address deforestation's root causes. On the contrary, most reports concluded that the plan had actually promoted deforestation and contributed to the deterioration of human living conditions (Colchester and Lohmann, 1990; Winterbottom, 1990; Shiva, 1987). Still, many tropical countries feared that these criticisms would jeopardize negotiations with international donors over TFAP activities.

It was under these uncertain conditions that the TFAP office in Guatemala held a roundtable discussion on project profiles with potential donors. Responding to international agencies, the director of TFAP-Guatemala (TFAP-G) was looking for ways to integrate ethnic minorities and NGOs into the planning process. On the other hand, the World Resources Institute (one of the plan's original proponents) wanted to demonstrate that criticisms of the TFAP could be addressed nationally if governments were willing to try.

In this spirit, TFAP-G and WRI asked the Academy of Mayan Languages of Guatemala (ALMG) to join the discussions. ALMG, a decentralized research institute within the Ministry of Education, is run by Maya speakers. Although ALMG is not a development agency, it is well connected to Mayan organizations throughout the country. Equally important, as part of the Ministry, it had government's approval—crucial because Guatemala was just emerging from decades of military rule, civil unrest, and repression of indigenous populations.

During meetings facilitated by WRI, representatives from ALMG and TFAP-G agreed that the roundtable might have more credibility if ALMG was represented, but that the move would do little to increase the Maya population's participation in planning. Accordingly, TFAP-G and ALMG agreed to start a far-reaching consultation to promote widespread Mayan involvement in the planning and implementation of activities to protect and conserve forest resources. This process was called the Forestry Action Plan-Maya (PAF-MAYA). ALMG agreed to temporarily house PAF-MAYA, while WRI and TFAP-G agreed to provide technical and financial assistance. Soon after, other international organizations, such as the Worldwide Fund for Nature (WWF), pledged additional funds.

Over the next ten months, a team of Maya workshop facilitators was assembled. The team made several promotional visits to Mayan organizations across the country and held seven

These conflicts will only intensify as local economies meld with market economies. For example, among some Zapotec communities in Mexico, otherwise successful forestry enterprises have been paralyzed over disputes on how to use the revenues. Elected community officers sensitive to the majority's needs often channel revenues from timber sales to public works in the "cabecera municipal" (the most densely populated settlement of the municipality). On the other hand, smaller, more recent settlements in outlying areas (known as "agencias") derive little or no benefits from timber operations. The power of the "cabecera municipal" rests on its capacity to dominate collective decisions through the election of officers. The power of the "agencias" stems from regional consultation workshops that included representatives from 16 linguistic groups in Guatemala. The more than 1,000 participants—representing communities, municipalities, and grassroots organizations—elected representatives to attend a national workshop in December 1992 to review and amend a draft report of the consultation written by the PAF-Maya technical team.

This degree of popular involvement in project planning and decision-making among the Maya-speaking population is unprecedented in Guatemala. Currently, PAF-Maya, with technical assistance from PAFT-G, is developing proposals to present to international donors. The TFAP-G will sponsor these proposals, but Maya organizations will manage and implement the resulting projects.

As important as popular involvement in the project has been, PAF-Maya's most significant achievement has been helping communities to organize and mobilize to improve forest management. After each regional workshop, participants were asked to report back to their constituencies on the results. Many communities then formed working groups to further discuss environmental protection and forestry activities, and such groups have begun small reforestation projects and environmental education activities on their own. Meanwhile, Maya-speaking radio stations have integrated forest conservation and environmental education into their programs.

Also important is the collaborative relationship that PAFT-G and the PAF-Maya have developed. Finding ways to complement and support each other, the two groups have accomplished much more working together than they could have independently. For TFAP-G, beginning work directly with the Maya populations would have been difficult: it lacked the extensive network and credibility that ALMG already had among Maya organizations. On the other hand, because PAFT-G is housed within the Ministry of Agriculture, PAF-Maya could hold workshops for more than two hundred participants without inviting the suspicions of the police and the army. In this context, ALMG could promote cultural unity and pride among the Maya people in Guatemala and quickly establish itself as one of the country's most prominent Maya organizations.

While building linkages among government agencies, GROs, and NGOs, it is important to cultivate independent forums—such as PAF-Maya—in which marginal groups can discuss and formulate policy and project proposals. That said, such dialogues are more likely to influence government policy-making if they are coordinated with an official initiative. Similarly, all participant agencies, institutions, and organizations must have a strong stake in the work. By searching for opportunities to match the interests of the poor with those of the government, policy dialogue will gradually increase and decision-making will become more democratic.

their location in the forested areas. When disputes on revenue allocations arise, they block access to the forest, closing down lumber mills and halting forest activities for months at a time.

Conflicting interests among grassroots groups also emerge between the landed and the landless, and between those who form strategic alliances with economic and political brokers and those who do not. Gender considerations come into play too. *(See Box 8.)* All of these differences affect the way decisions are made and the decisions themselves (Leslie and Paolisso, 1989; Schmidt, et al. 1977).

Box 8. Overcoming Gender Biases

Gender is one of the most pervasive factors underlying differences in decision-making and power in many societies. Among some indigenous communities in rural Mexico, Guatemala, and the Andes, where leaders are elected in community meetings and scrutinized by the population, only men vote and hold office. Gender-based differences in power are difficult to address. Many are sanctioned by cultural norms and accepted by men and women alike. Nonetheless, most societies tolerate exceptions to the norm, and these exceptions offer a starting point in the creation of more equitable decision-making.

In the consultation to formulate a Forest Action Plan for the Mayan communities of Guatemala (PAF-Maya), the issue of women's participation was successfully resolved by appealing to the exception to overcome the rule. In 1992, the government of Guatemala sponsored a consultation among the Maya communities to help involve ethnic minorities and NGOs in formulating and planning a national tropical forest action plan. It soon became clear, however, that getting women to attend regional workshops would be difficult. Both behavioral codes and the multiple responsibili-

ties of women in the household made overnight stays outside the community very difficult for them. The World Resources Institute (the international collaborator providing technical and financial support to PAF-Maya) pointed out that the consultation process had inadvertently been structured to deny women—important users of forest resources—significant input.

Looking for a way out of this dilemma, organizers tried to find exceptions to the rule that prevented women from spending the night outside the community. Older married women, it turned out, often spend one or even several nights away from home conducting marketing activities. The organizers of the consultation decided to ask some of these women to start women's groups in their communities to discuss the issues that their male counterparts were debating and to report their conclusions and recommendations to the regional forum. As women organized, several decided that it would be acceptable to travel in groups led by senior women with standing in the community. In this way, female participation grew but traditional norms were not directly challenged.

2. Influence, power, and access to decision-making are not equally distributed. As obvious as it might sound, this is a point that needs to be stated because decision-making processes rarely respond to the needs and interests of the less powerful and under-organized. In addition, the ability to influence decisions within a community is not equally distributed among its members. Community leaders of marginal populations are likely to be privileged, at least by local standards. They may have more schooling, more land than other members, and better access to marketing channels (Chambers, 1983). As shown in the cases of the Philippines Upland Development Project and the Fishermen Federation in Ecuador,

individuals in leadership positions often use their power to advance their own interests or those of their closest associates, often at the expense of the community they represent.

These differences in the distribution of power at the local level are often overlooked by NGOs and other development assistance agencies. A USAID study found that NGOs often take pains to identify interlocutors to work in project planning as a way to make projects more responsive to local needs. Involving these interlocutors makes implementation easier; but because they tend to belong to the group of those who were better off in their communities, the projects are biased in their favor and against the interests of the less privileged, especially the poorest 40 percent of the local population (Tendler, 1982). Governments face a similar situation when they encounter entrenched local elites while trying to decentralize. It is also true that bypassing privileged groups so as to involve the most marginal people can be disastrous, since the former can boycott projects and retaliate against weaker groups (Poffenberger, 1990; Kincaid, 1983; Meza, 1981). To break the entrenchment of special interest groups or local elites, care needs to be taken to set in place the proper checks and balances needed to ensure multi-stakeholder participation.

C. Empowerment Through Planning

Given the diversity of interests among the various groups with a stake in development, and the complex interplay between interests and power, building internal agreements for action to address common needs is the first step toward strengthening local capacities for effective participation. As recent experiences in grassroots development and natural resource management in Latin America and elsewhere show, such agreement can be engendered during planning if representatives of all key interest groups are involved.

Often, planning appears as a process in the exclusive domain of technocrats and other experts at the highest level of government. But in simple terms, planning means organizing to allocate resources to meet current and future needs. Whether through formal or informal organizations, autocratic or participatory means, people at

the grassroots level use vernacular planning processes to define their needs and to take the steps necessary to meet them.

Indian communities in Mesoamerica and the Andean region of South America have developed quite effective ways to identify, plan, and carry out activities that meet their collective needs. Community issues are discussed and decided in organized meetings, which are run by elected community leaders and attended by representatives from all households. It is expected that all participants provide input in the discussions, where options are assessed and decisions for action taken. Decisions are made by consensus—or near-consensus—and are binding for all. Culturally sanctioned means of carrying out plans include labor pooling (known as *minga* in the Andes and *tequio* in Oaxaca, Mexico) and cash or in-kind contributions by each household in the community. Enforcement takes the form of social recognition for households that consistently fulfill their duty, or ostracism, fines, or incarceration for those who do not contribute their labor to the community's well-being (Aguirre Beltrán, 1962; Wolf, 1957).

In peasant societies, and particularly among indigenous groups, planning does not necessarily include such Western components as those measured by quantitative analysis, detailed breakdowns on how multiple variables affect one outcome, complex relationships between abstract objectives and specific indicators of success, or precise programming over time. In the Andean region, for example, vernacular planning differs from the formal government planning processes in the following ways:

41

1. It is holistic. It requires an understanding of the totality, without breaking it down into its different components.

2. It is spontaneous and based on common sense. It does not rely on causal analysis or on the study of abstract processes, but on examples and analogies.

3. It is developed through verbal consensus. Unlike formal planning, which frequently requires lengthy documentation and written analysis, community planning in the Andes takes place through meetings and informal discussions, which include a great deal of redundancy and revisitation of issues until an elected authority is able to express the consensus again verbally.

4. The activities to be carried out and the products expected are defined precisely; the schedule is not. While in vernacular planning expected outputs are clearly set, the schedule or timing is left vague to allow enough flexibility to adapt to the rhythm of rural life (Ramón, 1993).

Participatory Rural Appraisal (PRA) (GEA/WRI 1993; WRI, 1991; Conway, 1989), Planeamiento Andino Comunitario (PAC) (Ramón, 1993), and other community planning methodologies can be used to build local participation and negotiation capacities. PRA consists of loosely structured field inquiries and discussion aimed at defining local problems, opportunities, and actions to address the problems identified. PRA teams of 8 to 15 persons include both leaders and grassroots representatives (women among them), technical advisors, and government officials from various institutions and fields. In PRA, diagrams (such as community maps, transects, agronomic calendars, diagrams depicting local organizations and outside institutions, and flow charts) are used to help participants gather, organize, and analyze information so that problems and opportunities can be assessed. Typically, PRAs last ten days, during which the PRA team alternates field visits with group analysis and discussion.

Conflict resolution and consensus building are at the core of PRA. Because they represent various interests, PRA team members frequently disagree on how to interpret specific information. These disagreements, phrased as questions that can be answered through additional fieldwork, are used as opportunities to build consensus within the PRA team. Findings are then presented to the community in an open meeting, where they are reviewed and amended, where problems and actions are ranked, and where action plans are drafted.

In PRA, local team members contribute their knowledge on local practices, facilitate interaction with other villagers, and help identify actions that will catalyze community consensus. Outsiders, for their part, have ample opportunities to ask questions and voice their own insights, which tend to be technical. When problems and solutions are ranked, outside specialists pitch in information to help communities assess the feasibility of proposals. Sometimes, additional expertise is needed in more specialized assessments or in training local people on specific topics. *(See Box 9.)*

A key challenge of participatory planning is to integrate vernacular planning processes with formal planning systems to make them more inclusive and to improve their results.

D. When Western Meets Vernacular

Even though vernacular planning—namely, actions traditionally undertaken by some communities to address collective needs—meets their overall needs, interests are so diverse and power differences among marginal populations so great that women and the very poor are often excluded. Furthermore, even when vernacular planning and organization reflect consensus, this consensus is often articulated only verbally or in ways that strike the outsider as cryptic. Rarely are commu-

Box 9. Galvanizing Popular Will for Action

In Guatemala's Chiquimulas region, the World Resources Institute, the Asociación de Entidades de Desarrollo y de Servicio No Gubernamentales de Guatemala (ASINDES) and the office of the National Tropical Forest Action Plan (TFAP-G) carried out a PRA to promote local participation in project planning and the implementation of the Tropical Forest Action Plan (TFAP). The PRA team included men and women representing three local villages, as well as staff from ASINDES, TFAP-G, and other NGOs working in Chiquimulas. During the PRA, participants agreed that poor forest management practices have led to rapid deforestation, soil erosion, and fuelwood scarcity. Everyone agreed that these problems hurt the region as a whole and that, if these trends continued, their children would face a much harder situation. This was not news to the people, but before the PRA not much had been done to change matters either.

The PRA helped galvanize local will for action. Since the three villages faced similar problems, community representatives decided to form a regional organization to promote the formation and coordination of three community forest committees. These village committees were given responsibility for protecting the forest—controlling tree diseases, reforesting, and monitoring tree cutting.

Local representatives told the TFAP office that they would bear all the costs of forest protection and reforestation if the TFAP office would train community members in the basics of forest protection, seedling production, and nursery management. The proposal proved very attractive to the TFAP office, which soon dispatched technicians to train the village forestry committees. But demands for training were high, and the TFAP office lacked the staff to do the job itself. Thus, a "trainer of trainers" approach was developed, whereby the TPAF-G trained local volunteers, who, in turn, trained the village committees.

The Chiquimulas PRA helped galvanize local communities around issues that affected them all, triggering a process of social organization that built on existing institutions. The result has been a win-win situation. TFAP-G has been able to involve local communities in improved forest management and protection at a very small cost while the communities have gained the technical support needed to address important needs without relinquishing control over their resources and their activities.

nity decisions backed by data and facts that can satisfy the requirements of other interested parties, such as governmental bodies, merchants, or development agencies. This severely undermines the ability of the grassroots groups to negotiate.

A key challenge of participatory planning is to integrate vernacular planning processes with formal planning systems to make them more inclusive and to improve their results. Formal planning systems should include methods and tools that can help empower marginal populations by incorporating traditional and technical knowledge into action plans and ensure that these plans will be consistent not only with identified needs but with the culture and social fabric of the community. In turn, vernacular planning must ensure that the needs of marginal populations within the community are incorporated into planning, that decisions are well understood by all participants in planning exercises, and that both needs and proposed actions are properly communicated to relevant outsiders (governments, development agencies, etc.)—all of which is likely to strengthen all parties' commitment to the implementation of plans.

The integration of formal and vernacular planning elements has a precedent in Andean Community Planning (PAC), a methodology developed by COMUNIDEC (an Ecuadorean NGO that supports grassroots organizations) and the World Resources Institute while seeking indigenous people's participation in the TFAP in the Province of Bolívar, Ecuador. PAC is a bottom-up micro-regional planning method that addresses community needs while strengthening self-help capacities. It also facilitates negotiations between small localities and the regional authorities on development and environmental issues. PAC is sensitive to the traditional ways in which populations plan, but also responds to the requirements of government agencies, donors, and others.

PAC consists of a series of community planning workshops that feed into a micro-regional planning workshop. Developed through trial and error, the approach includes focus-group discussions as well as field testing and modification over 18 months. Ten simple instruments are used to help villagers analyze the economic and social aspects of natural resource management. PAC's brief written guidelines lead participants to chart a thumbnail history of the community and the land, prepare community maps and a calendar, describe their local institutions, make farm sketches and identify methods of agricultural production, map out relations with brokers, identify self-help groups within the community, and make use of existing community action plans. Using these instruments, villagers can analyze the social and economic relationships within the community, as well as those between the community and the broader society, and can assess problems, resources, and options for improving local natural resource management. *(See Box 10.)*

Box 10. Similar Problems, Different Priorities

While seeking indigenous people's participation in the TFAP in the Province of Bolívar in Ecuador, the World Resources Institute and COMUNIDEC faced a dilemma. Well-organized communities capable of defining and addressing their priorities were much less capable of coordinating with other communities to tackle common problems. In this case, micro-regional coordination appeared efficient since the communities involved faced very similar problems that required similar solutions. It also seemed cost effective since communities in each micro-region were already organized into federations. At the same time, for administrative reasons donors were more interested in funding a few micro-regional projects than many community projects (Cabarle and Zazueta, 1992).

The challenge in this case was twofold. One need was to design a program that genuinely met local needs and drew on the community's strong organizational and planning skills. The other was to incorporate federations into the project to facilitate administration, reduce costs by avoiding duplication, and coordinate the exchange of lessons and experiences among different communities.

To address this challenge, COMUNIDEC cooperated with the region's five federations—which involved 205 communities—to develop, test, and apply PAC. First, federation officials and outside collaborators visited each community to explain the project's purpose and to invite participation. Then communities were given roughly two weeks to discuss and respond to the invitation. Once they agreed to participate, communities were asked to appoint a village committee of 10 individuals (including leaders, women, youth, kinship groups, etc.) to assess problems, propose solutions, and take responsibility for implementing and following up PAC. These village committees were then invited to a two-day training workshop where they were introduced to

Box 10. (continued)

PAC's community planning method and participated in a PAC exercise.

Back home, using a PAC handbook as a planning guide, each village committee ran a two-day PAC workshop to identify (but not rank) the community's most prevalent problems, along with activities to address them. Using drawings, the village committee presented its assessment and recommendations in an open community meeting. Once workshop participants gave feedback on and modified both, problems and actions were ranked and the community formally adopted these priorities as its action plan.

The issues and proposals that the village committees identified in this way were few, simple, and straightforward. In the village of Puchi Guallavin, for instance, the committee proposed a one-year action plan—seven activities tied to very concrete targets, such as reducing deforestation by planting 150,000 trees and controlling soil erosion by building soil-erosion ditches on 8 hectares.

In most of the 205 villages where PAC was tested, existing plans were compared with the new plan developed by the village committee through PAC. In most cases, the new proposals were approved easily in community meetings because deviations from the old plans that represented a community consensus before the PAC workshop took place were easy to spot, discuss, and resolve. On the other hand, the community often changed the targets proposed by the village committees. Specifically, the scope of work was often reduced and made more specific. In Puchi Guallavin, the types of activities suggested were approved by the community, but the proposed targets were dramatically reduced. Reforestation activities were reduced from 150,000 to 124,000 trees, and the number of the trees of each species was specified. The amount of land to be protected by erosion-prevention ditches was decreased from 8 to 4 hectares.

In PAC's second phase, a micro-regional plan was elaborated to put local interests in the context of a somewhat larger region. An aggregate plan is then developed based on the interests expressed in community plans. To prepare for the micro-regional planning workshop, each community submitted its plan to federation officials, who incorporated such key information on the micro-region as the location of settlements, the availability of infrastructure, and potential collaborating institutions. The plan and background information were distributed to workshop participants, including federation officials, community officials, village committees and representatives of collaborating agencies. At planning workshops, the similarities and differences in the problems and solutions proposed by the various communities were identified, training needs were spelled out, a new overall budget was developed, and the phases for implementing the plan were defined.

In this process, community representatives were given the task of synthesizing community plans, compelling them to learn about each other's needs and intentions. Once village representatives realized that they had many problems in common, they identified several activities that federations could carry out to help implement the plans, the final versions of which were ratified in a community meeting.

Through this bottom-up approach, five micro-regional projects were formulated to respond to community priorities and allow villages to retain control of most project activities. In one micro-regional workshop, community representatives named deforestation, soil erosion, and drought as their most pressing problems. To address soil erosion and deforestation, village committees were made responsible for making erosion-control improvements in 10 percent of agricultural lands and for reforesting 15 percent of lands not currently in use. The federation was given support tasks, such

Box 10. continued

as organizing workshops to train community extensionists on nursery management and techniques for controlling soil erosion, setting up field visits, and purchasing and distributing tools to the village committees (Ramón, 1993). To address problems caused by drought, federations decided to purchase small pumps for each community and to ask the government to conduct an irrigation-feasibility study for the region. Operation of pumping equipment was left to the village committees.

Although a key purpose of micro-regional planning was to promote intercommunal collaboration on the basis of common needs, PAC did not overlook each community's particular needs. For some, the priority was to build a health center. For others, public laundries were identified as an item that would make women's lives easier. The construction of a community center also ranked high on the agenda of some other villages (Ramón, 1993).

The PAC process was carried out largely by villagers. COMUNIDEC's role was to develop and test PAC, train village committees on its use, facilitate the micro-regional workshops, and help draft the final micro-regional plans. The five federations submitted their plans for funding to the Dutch government as a US$2 million project of the Ecuadorean TFAP and received funding.

PAC helped people reach consensus on the key elements of micro-regional project proposals, responded to local needs, and kept decision-making and program implementation within the community. Drawing heavily on elected officials and existing micro-regional federations, customs (community meetings), and vernacular planning, PAC also innovated in ways that made the planning process more accountable and efficient. By establishing a village committee and insisting that its diagnosis of the community's main problems be discussed in open meetings attended by villagers, PAC broadened participation in decision-making beyond elected officials. This bottom-up approach also introduced into the early stages of project planning a healthy and lasting local bias in the analysis of needs, priorities, and means of implementation.

Flexibility in developing and applying PAC was key to its success. Initially, planning workshops included five days of intensive field visits and discussions by village committees. During the initial training workshops, however, it became apparent that few community members could spare five days away from their regular occupations. At the same time, organizers learned that most communities had already developed priorities and in many cases had reached consensus or had to address them. Since villages had their own vernacular plans, organizers shifted the focus of workshops to participatory analysis and review of existing action plans and scaled the meeting down to two days.

The PAC planning process yielded clearly defined objectives, activities, and expected actions, including a quick but convincing analysis of local conditions that justified the choice of certain development activities over others. Aware of the donors' need for an agile mechanism to administer funds, PAC participants were able to turn their federations—previously viewed with distrust and skepticism—into assets by assigning them clearly defined roles, such as coordinating training workshops and purchasing tools wholesale, that facilitated project implementation.

In summary, planning methods such as PRA and PAC help ensure both greater community participation in decision-making and a more open political process. These tools also improve people's capacities to analyze information and help build their support for decisions on project planning and implementation. Methods such as PRA and PAC also strengthen the negotiation capacities of local communities in their interaction with governments, NGOs, and donors by helping them to clearly articulate a local consensus for action.

Because these methods tend to rely on local organizations, knowledge, and capabilities, they are likely to result in proposals and actions that the communities themselves can carry out, provided that they get the external resources they need. Empowering communities to retain control of their own development also significantly reduces the burden on government. Nonetheless, government involvement in participatory planning is important because through processes such as PAC or PRA officials can learn how to make policies and programs more responsive to the needs and objectives of marginal populations.

V. Conclusion

The consensus emerging over the last few years is that environmentally sound development and equitable economic development go hand in hand. Similarly, it is now widely accepted that neither can occur if participatory democracy is not strengthened. Pressures from the grassroots, as well as from international cooperation agencies, bilateral and multilateral development bodies, and international financial institutions, have prompted many governments to sanction civil society's participation in planning and carrying out sustainable development.

Obviously, the degree of participation and the opportunities for change will vary from place to place. It is also certain that development will become more democratic—a three-steps-forward two-steps-back exercise along an uncharted road filled with obstacles. The biggest challenge is to transform the decision-making structures and processes that have evolved to further the interests and objectives of the powerful and the status quo. These vehicles of sustainable development must become flexible enough to involve new interest groups and stakeholders in bargaining over resource use, allocation, and distribution.

New fiscal and administrative realities facing the public sector, as well as a stronger, better organized, and more active civil society, are driving the search for the new forms of governance that will, in turn, make environmental policy-making more equitable and participatory. In them, the state and its citizens share governance responsibilities. In this drive to put the concept of participation into practice, governments must:

1. Restructure, building more and better mechanisms for listening to and consulting with various stakeholders before policies are adopted or reformed.

The use of governing and advisory boards, steering committees, consultation forums, and public audiences when policies are formulated and projects are implemented will boost stakeholder participation in sustainable development.

2. Form new alliances among groups that have been excluded from decision- and policy-making.

This process will entail building the capacities of marginal populations to propose and negotiate actions and policies that meet their needs. By strengthening new constituencies, governments will check and balance the dominant sectors likely to oppose change. An additional benefit: governments will have a broader and more secure power base.

3. Make information easily available to policy-makers, citizens groups, and the general public.

By contributing to enlightened participation, this will lead to better informed decisions. The implementation of "right to know" legislation, which provides a legal basis for citizens groups to hold public agencies and private enterprises accountable on environmental issues affecting public welfare, will certainly help strengthen this process. So will organizing information clearly and developing the institutional mechanisms needed to act on environmental complaints from citizen groups.

Clearly, government has a catalytic role to play in creating new, more democratic, and flexible policy-making institutions, structures, and methods; in developing the negotiation capacities of marginal groups; and in making available the information needed for informed choices.

The tasks ahead are not easy. Responding to new interests—most of which will compete with those of well-established powerful groups—will require a new set of skills in the art of governing. Mediating, facilitating, coordinating, and catalyzing consensus-building will become all important. The good news is that this may be the role that governments have been searching for in the aftermath of the debt crisis and structural adjustment since the crisis was triggered partly by unrealistically high expectations about government's financial and administrative abilities to directly address social, environmental, and economic needs by providing services, managing natural resources, and getting directly involved in production and marketing activities. As many of these functions devolve to civil society, an opportunity emerges to enhance participatory democracies and search for administrative structures that can make better use of available financial, human, organizational, and cultural resources while allowing governments to focus on monitoring policy, regulation, and compliance and enforcement. Yet, this devolution will probably fail unless citizens groups are given not just new responsibilities, but also new financial, institutional, and political support.

As for civil society, its main responsibility is to remain the force behind this government change. Citizens' organizations have the duty to:

1. Practice responsible participation.

Citizens' organizations must continue to press governments for greater openness, accountability, and participation in decision-making and in the implementation of decisions. Specifically, citizens' organizations must learn to participate more constructively—not just making demands but also identifying opportunities and striving to make participation work. Here both the willingness and the capacity to build partnerships among themselves and with government institutions are critical. Making more realistic proposals that take into account the views and interests of various sectors within society will help them to gain both official respect and support.

Bridges must be extended between governments and their new constituencies so that opposition can be turned into propositions and confrontation into negotiation.

2. Build the capacity to deliver services once delivered by governments.

While considerable organizational resources within civil society can be mobilized to improve service delivery or to perform tasks previously seen as governments' exclusive responsibilities, NGOs, grassroots groups, and other organizations must improve the managerial and technical capacities that will allow them to help resolve specific problems. Upgrading their skills will also help them better understand the problems and the range of possible solutions. Once they have a good track record, their credibility and respect will rise among skeptical government officials and stakeholders.

3. Keep the general public informed.

Non-governmental organizations, universities, and research centers have already become alternative sources of information on development and environmental policies, helping citizens take on the responsibilities that come with participation in policy-making. The ability of NGOs and other independent institutions to understand and work with the mass media, as well as their knowledge and use of modern communications technologies (especially electronic mail and networks), will allow them to help open up participation in policy-making to a broader range of interests.

In most developing regions, and certainly in Latin America, governments have traditionally viewed independent organizations as a threat to be subdued. Cultural biases and prejudices against the poor and ethnic minorities feed this belief. Conversely, grassroots and other independent organizations have long viewed government as an anti-democratic authority to be challenged and opposed. Against this backdrop, bridges must be extended between governments and their new constituencies so that opposition can be turned into propositions and confrontation into negotiation. At the same time, all parties must begin to accept each other as indispensable partners in sustainable development.

Dr. Aarón Zazueta is an anthropologist who has been working for more than ten years in community development and environmental policy issues in Latin America. He works with grassroots groups, local communities, NGOs, and governments to develop methods and institutions for strengthening participation in decision-making.

References

Aguirre Beltrán, Gonzalo. 1962. *Regiones de Refugio: El desarrollo de la comunidad y el proceso dominical en Mestizoamérica*. Mexico: Ed. del INI.

Annis, Sheldon, Oscar Arias, James D. Nations, Stephen B. Cox, Alvaro Umaña, Katrina Brandon, Stuart K. Tucker, John D. Strasma, and Rafael Celis. 1992. *Poverty, Natural Resources and Public Policy in Central America*. New Brunswick, New Jersey: Transaction Publishers.

Archibold, Guillermo. 1992. "Pemasky in Kuna Yala." In Valerie Barzetti and Yanina Rovinski (eds.), *Toward a Green Central America*. New Haven, Connecticut: Kumarian Press.

Bagadion, Benjamin U. and Frances F. Korten. 1991. "Developing Irrigators' Organizations: A Learning Process Approach." In Mitchell M. Cernea (ed.), *Putting People First*. 2nd edition. London: Oxford University Press.

Bartra, Armando, Manolo Fernández, Jonathan Fox, Gustavo Gordillo, Luis Hernández, Gonzalo Chapela, Francisco Pérez Arce, Isabel Cruz, Martín Zuvire, Ana de Ita, Patricia Gérez and Julio Moguel. 1991. *Los Nuevos Sujetos del Desarrollo Rural*. Mexico: ADN Editores.

Bebbington, Anthony. 1991. "Sharecropping Agricultural Development: The Potential for GSO-Government Cooperation." *Grassroots Development*, 15/2

Bebbington, Anthony, Galo Ramón, Hernán Carrasco, Víctor Hugo Torres, Lourdes Peralvo and Jorge Trujillo. 1992a. *Actores de una Década Ganada: Tribus, Comunidades, y Campesinos en la Modernidad*. Quito: COMUNIDEC.

Bebbington, Anthony, Hernán Carrasco, Lourdes Peralbo, Galo Ramón, Victor Hugo Torres and Jorge Trujillo. 1992. "From Protest to Productivity: The Evolution of Indigenous Federations in Ecuador." *Grassroots Development*, 16/2.

Benjamin, Thomas. 1989. *A Rich Land, A Poor People*. Albuquerque, New Mexico: University of New Mexico Press.

Bray, David Barton. 1991. "The Struggle for the Forest: Conservation and Development in the Sierra Juárez." *Grassroots Development*, 15/3.

Bray, David Barton, Marcelo Carreón, Leticia Merino and Victoria Santos. 1993. "On the Road to Sustainable Forestry: The Maya of Quintana Roo are striving to combine economic efficiency, ecological sustainability, and a democratic society." *Cultural Survival Quarterly*, Spring.

Bunch, Roland. 1990. "Encouraging Farmers' Experiments." In Robert Chambers, Arnold Pacey and Lori Ann Thrupp (eds.), *Farmer First: Farmer Innovation and Agricultural Research*. London: Intermediate Technology Publications.

53

Cabarle, Bruce J. 1991. "Community Forestry and the Social Ecology of Development." *Grassroots Development*, 15/3.

Cabarle, Bruce and Aaron Zazueta. 1992. "Gaining Ground: People's Participation in the Tropical Forest Action Plan for Ecuador." *Forests, Trees and People Newsletter*, No. 15/16.

Cabarle, Bruce J., Manuel Huaya Panduro and Oswaldo Manihuari Murayari. 1993. *Ecofarming in the Peruvian Amazon: The Integrated Family and Communal Garden Project (HIFCO)*. Prepared for the Liz Claiborne-Art Ortenberg Foundation Community-Based Workshop, Arlie, VA, October 18–22, 1993.

Carroll, Thomas F. 1992. *Intermediary NGOs: The Supporting Link in Grassroots Development*. Hartford, Connecticut: Kumarian Press.

Castro, Ma. Eugenia and Elvira Flores. 1992–93. *Fomento Solidario a la Vivienda, FOSOVI A.C., estudio de caso*. Prepared for "Taller de Experiencias en Procesos Participativos de Problemas Urbanos y Ambientales." Mexico, D.F., 1/20/94.

Central American Commission on Environment and Development (CCAD). 1992. *Central American Agenda on Environment and Development*. Guatemala: CCAD.

Cernea, Michael M. 1992. *The Building Blocks of Participation: Testing Bottom-Up Planning*. 1992. World Bank Discussion Paper no. 166. Washington, D.C.: The World Bank

Cernea, Michael M. (ed.). 1991. *Putting People First: Sociological Variables in Rural Development*. New York: Oxford University Press.

Chambers, Robert. 1983. *Rural Development: Putting the Last First*. Langman, Harlow

Chambers, Robert, Arnold Pacey and Lori Ann Thrupp (eds.). 1989. *Farmer First: Farmer Innovation and Agricultural Research*. London: Intermediate Technology Publications.

Chapela, Gonzalo. 1992. "Nueva ley forestal, nuevo interlocutor." *Cuadernos Agrarios, 27 Constitucional*. Nueva época, año 2, núm. 5–6, mayo-diciembre. Mexico: Federación Editorial Mexicana.

Colchester, Marcus, and Larry Lohmann. 1990. "The Tropical Forestry Action Plan: What Progress?" London: World Rainforest Movement, The Ecologist, Friends of the Earth.

Conway, Gordon R. 1989. "Diagrams for Farmers." In Robert Chambers, Arnold Pacey and Lori Ann Thrupp (eds.), *Farmer First: Farmer Innovation and Agricultural Research*. London: Intermediate Technology Publications.

CPNAB. April 1993. "El Consejo de Pueblos Nahuas del Alto Balsas (CPNAB), Los Primeros Años: 1989–1992." *Cuadernos de Alto Balsas No.1*. Mexico: Grupo de Estudios Ambientales, A.C.

CPNAB-GEA. April 1993. "Hacia un camino propio de los pueblos del Alto Balsas: síntesis del proyecto alternativo CPNAB-GEA." *Cuadernos de Alto Balsas No.2*. Mexico: Grupo de Estudios Ambientales, A.C.

Cuadernos Agrarios, 27 Constitucional. Nueva época, año 2, núm. 5–6, mayo-diciembre 1992. Mexico: Federación Editorial Mexicana.

Dorm-Abzobu, Clement, Okeame Ampadu-Agyei and Peter G. Veit. 1991. *Religious Beliefs and Environmental Protection: The Malshegu Sacred Grove in Northern Ghana*. Washington, D.C.: World Resources Institute, and Nairobi, Kenya: Acts Press, African Center for Technology Studies.

Dourojeanni, Marc J. 1982. *Renewable Natural Resources of Latin America and the Caribbean: Situation and Trends*. Washington, D.C.: World Wildlife Federation.

Durning, Alan. 1990. "Ending Poverty." In Lester Brown, Alan Durning, Christopher Flavin, Hilary French, Jodi Jacobson, Marcia Lowe, Sandra Postel, Michael Renner, Linda Starke, and John Young (eds.), *State of the World: A Worldwatch In-*

stitute Report on Progress Toward a Sustainable Society. New York: W.W. Norton & Company.

Environmental and Energy Study Institute Task Force. 1991. *Partnership for Sustainable Development: A New U.S. Agenda for International Development and Environmental Security*. Washington, D.C.: Environmental and Energy Study Institute.

EWLA (Environment Watch: Latin America). 1994. *Chile's Environmental Framework Law Awaits President's Signature*. February 1994.

Esteva, Joaquin. 1994. *La Restauración de una Cuenca Lacutre en México y el Proceso Participativo Social Regional. El Caso de la ORCA*. Mexico: Pátzcuaro-Michoacán, Mexico: CESE, WRI.

Farnsworth, Edward G. 1991. "The Inter-American Development Bank's Integration with Non-Governmental Environmental Organizations." *Third Conference on the Environment: Consultations with Public Agencies and Non-Governmental Organizations concerned with Environmental Protection and Conservation of Natural Resources in Latin America and the Caribbean*. Caracas, Venezuela.

Farrington, John, and Anthony Bebbington, with Kate Wellard and David J. Lewis. 1993. *Reluctant Partners: Non-Governmental Organizations, the State and Sustainable Agricultural Development*. New York: Routledge.

Forester, John. 1980. "Critical Theory and Planning Practice." *APA Journal*, July.

Fox, Jonathan. 1992. "Democratic Rural Development: Leadership Accountability in Regional Peasant Organizations." In Martin Doornbos, Henk van Roosmalen and Ashwani Saith (eds.), *Development and Change*, 23/2.

Fox, Jonathan and Gustavo Gordillo. 1991. "Entre el Estado y el mercado: perspectivas para un desarrollo autónomo en el campo mexicano." In Armando Bartra, Manolo Fernández, Jonathan Fox, Gustavo Gordillo, Luis Hernán-

dez, Gonzalo Chapela, Francisco Pérez Arce, Isabel Cruz, Martín Zuvire, Ana de Ita, Patricia Gérez and Julio Moguel (eds.), *Los Nuevos Sujetos del Desarrollo Rural*. Mexico: ADN Editores.

Fox, Jonathan and Luis Hernández. 1989. "Offsetting the Iron Law of Oligarchy: The Ebb and Flow of Leadership Accountability in a Regional Peasant Organization." *Grassroots Development*, 13/2.

Freeman, Peter H. 1991. "Environmental Impact Assessments in the Inter-American Development Bank's Lending Program." *Third Conference on the Environment: Consultations with Public Agencies and Non-Governmental Organizations Concerned With Environmental Protection and Conservation of Natural Resources in Latin America and the Caribbean*. Caracas, Venezuela.

Freire, Paulo. 1969. *Pedagogía del Oprimido*. Mexico: Siglo Veintiuno Editores, S.A.

Fujisaka, Sam. 1990. "Rainfed Lowland Rice: Building Research On Farmer Practice and Technical Knowledge." *Agriculture, Ecosystems and Environment, No. 33*. Amsterdam: Elsevier Science Publishers.

GEA/WRI (Grupo de Estudios Ambientales, A.C./World Resources Institute). 1993. *El proceso de Evaluación Rural Participativa: una propuesta metodológica*. August, 1993.

IDB/UNDP (Inter-American Development Bank/ United Nations Development Programme). 1990. *Our Own Agenda*. Washington, D.C./ New York, NY.

Kaimowitz, David. 1993. "The Role of Nongovernmental Organizations in Agricultural Research and Technology Transfer in Latin America." *World Development*, vol. 21, no. 7.

Kincaid, Douglas. 1983. "Honduras: Rural Politics and Agrarian Reform I-IV. *Mesoamerica*, 2/5, May–October.

Korten, David C. 1980. "Community Organizations and Rural Development: A Learning Process Approach." *Development Methods*, Sept./Oct. 1980.

Kottak, Conrad Phillip. 1991. "When People Don't Come First: Some Sociological Lessons from Completed Projects." In Michael M. Cernea (ed.), *Putting People First: Sociological Variables in Rural Development*. New York: Oxford University Press.

Leonard, H. Jeffrey. 1989. *Remedies are Available for Latin America's Environmental Ills*. Washington, D.C.: Conservation Foundation Letter.

Leslie, Joanne, and Michael Paolisso. 1989. *Women, Work, and Child Welfare in the Third World*. Boulder, Colorado: Westview Press.

López Arzola, Rodolfo y Patricia Gérez Fernández. 1993. "The Permanent Tension." *Cultural Survival Quarterly*, Spring.

MacDonald, Ted. 1992. "Working with Indigenous Peoples in Latin America: Towards Social Equity in the Conservation of Fragile Lands and Protected Areas." *Cultural Survival*.

Mexico & NAFTA Report. "President Salinas changes strategy: Jaw jaw rather than war war." February 24, 1994.

Meza, Victor. 1981. *Política y Sociedad en Honduras*. Tegucigalpa: Editorial Guaymuras.

Moguel, Julio. 1990. "El Programa Nacional de Solidaridad, ¿para quién?" *El Cotidiano: Revista de la Realidad Mexicana Actual No. 38*. Mexico: Universidad Autónoma Metropolitana.

Moguel, Julio, Carlota Botey y Luis Hernández (eds.). 1992. *Autonomía y Nuevos Sujetos Sociales en el Desarrollo Rural*. Mexico: Siglo Veintiuno Editores, S.A. de C.V.

MOPU (Ministerio de Obras Públicas). 1990. *Desarrollo y Medio Ambiente en América Latina: Una Visión Evolutiva*. Madrid: MOPU.

Morss, Elliot R. and George H. Hondale. 1985. "Differing Agendas." In Elliot R. Morss and David Gow (eds.), *Implementing Rural Development Projects: Lessons from AID and World Bank Experiences*. London: Westview Press.

National Environment Secretariat of Kenya, Egerton University of Kenya, Clark University and Center for International Development and Environment of the World Resources Institute. 1990. *Participatory Rural Appraisal Handbook: Conducting PRAs in Kenya*. Washington, D.C.: World Resources Institute.

OECD (Organization for Economic Cooperation and Development). 1991. *The State of the Environment*. Paris: OECD Publications Service.

Painter, Michael and William H. Durham, eds. 1995. *The Social Causes of Environmental Destruction in Latin America*. Ann Arbor, Univ. of Michigan Press.

"Participación Popular para una Sociedad más Justa y Solidaria." In Boletín Financiero No 2. Febrero 1995.

Perfil de La Jornada. "Compromisos por la Paz." 3/3/94.

Poffenberger, Mark. 1990. *Keepers of the Forest: Land Management Alternatives in Southeast Asia*. West Hartford, Connecticut: Kumarian Press.

Poole, Peter. 1989. *Developing a Partnership of Indigenous Peoples, Conservationists, and Land Use Planners in Latin America*. Washington, D.C.: The World Bank, Latin American and Caribbean Technical Department.

Posey, Darrel. 1993. "Alternatives to Forest Destruction. Lessons from the Mêbêngokrê Indians." In Susan E. Place (ed.), *Tropical Rainforests, Latin America's Nature and Society in Transition*. Wilmington, DE: Jaguar Books.

Presidencia de la República de Bolivia. Febrero 1992. "Taller de Consulta: Conformación del

Consejo Administrativo de la Cuenca Iniciativa para las Americas"

PROAFT (Programa de Acción Forestal Tropical, A.C.). 1993. *Boletín Informativo*, May 1993.

Pryjomko, Roman. 1993. *African Wildlife Management Challenges GIS*. Fort Collins, CO: GIS World Inc.

Ramón Valarezo, Galo. 1993. *Manual de Planeamiento Andino Comunitario. El PAC en la Región Andina*. Quito, Ecuador: COMUNIDEC, WRI, FAO.

Rocheleau, Dianne E. 1991. "Participatory Research in Agroforestry: Learning from Experience and Expanding our Repertoire." *Agroforestry Systems, No. 15*. Netherlands: Kluwer Academic Publishers.

de los Reyes, Romana and Sylvia G. Jopillo. 1986. *An Evaluation of the Philippine Participatory Communal Irrigation Program*. Philippines: Institute of Philippine Culture.

Rhoades, Robert E. and Robert Booth. 1982. *Farmer Back to the Farmer: A Model for Generating Acceptable Agricultural Technology*. Agricultural Administration.

Saunier, Robert E. and Stephen O. Bender. 1988. *The Urban Dimension of Environmental Concern in Latin America and the Caribbean*. Washington, D.C.: Organization of American States, Department of Regional Development.

Schacter, Mark. 1989. *Bolivia's "Emergency Social Fund": Historical Notes and Impressions*. Presented at World Bank Seminar Series, "Bolivia's Emergency Social Fund: Alleviating the Social Cost of (Non) Adjustment." September 26–27, 1989.

Schmidt, Steffen W., James C. Scott, Carl Landé and Laura Guasti (eds.). 1977. *Friends, Followers and Factions: A Reader in Political Clientelism*. Berkeley, California: University of California Press.

Secretaría de Desarrollo Social, Instituto Nacional de Ecología (SEDESOL). 1993. *México: Informe de la Situación General en Materia de Equilibrio Ecológico y Protección al Ambiente 1993–1994*. Secretaría de Desarrollo Social.

Servicios de Educación de Adultos, A.C./Fundación Friedrich Ebert (SEDAC/FFE). 1992. *Establos Colectivos: Del Autodidactismo a la Autogestión*. Mexico: SEDAC/FFE.

Secretaría General del Medio Ambiente (SEGMA), 1993. *Planificación y gestión del medio ambiente: políticas e instrumentos*. La Paz, Bolivia: Artes Gráficas Latina.

Shiva, Vandana. 1987. *Forestry Crisis and Forestry Myths: A Critical Review of Tropical Forests: A Call to Action*. Penang, Malaysia: World Rainforest Movement.

Slayter, B. Thomas, C. Kabutha, and R. Ford. 1991. *Traditional Village Institutions in Environmental Management: Erosion Control in Katheka, Kenya*. Washington, D.C.: World Resources Institute, and Nairobi, Kenya: Acts Press, African Center for Technology Studies.

Stern, Alissa. 1993. "Taking Charge: The tactics of the Indonesian environmental agency are beginnning to impact on business despite a lack of regulatory power." *Environment Risk*. London: Euromoney Publications.

Tamang, Devika. 1993. *Living in a Fragile Ecosystem: Indigenous Soil Management in the Hills of Nepal*, Gatekeeper Series No. 41. International Institute for Environment and Development.

Tendler, Judith. 1982. "Turning Private Voluntary Organizations into Development Agencies: Questions for Evaluation." *A.I.D. Program Evaluation Discussion Paper No. 12*. Washington, D.C.: U.S. Agency for International Development.

Thrupp, Lori Ann. 1989. "Legitimizing Local Knowledge: From Displacement to Empowerment for Third World People." *Agriculture and Human Values*. Summer 1989.

United Nations Conference on Environment and Development (UNCED). 1993. *Agenda 21*. New York, NY.

United Nations Environmental Program (UNEP). 1989. *Environmental Data Report, second edition*. Cambridge, England: Blackwell.

Uphoff, Norman. 1993. "Grassroots Organizations and NGOs in Rural Development: Opportunities with Diminishing States and Expanding Markets." *World Development*, vol. 21, no. 4.

——. 1986. *Local Institutional Development: An Analytical Sourcebook with Cases*. Ithaca, New York: Kumarian Press.

Van Sant, Jerry. 1987. "Benefit Sustainability." Prepared for the Advisory Committee for Voluntary Foreign Aid. Washington, D.C.: Development Alternatives, Inc.

Winders, David. 1992. *From Timber Concession to Community Forestry: Political, Economic and Social Changes in the Sierra Juárez, Oaxaca, México*. Paper presented to the Latin American Seminar, St. Anthony's College, Oxford University, October 1992.

Winterbottom, Robert. 1990. *Taking Stock: The Tropical Forestry Action Plan After Five Years*. Washington, DC: World Resources Institute.

Wolf, Eric R. 1957. "Closed Corporate Peasant Communities in Mesoamerica and Central Java." *Southwestern Journal of Anthropology*, No. 13.

——. 1956. "Aspects of Group Relations in a Complex Society." *American Anthropologist*, No. 58.

World Bank. 1992. *Environment and Development in Latin America and the Caribbean: The Role of the World Bank*. Washington, D.C.

——. 1992(a). *World Development Report 1992: Development and the Environment*. London: Oxford University Press.

World Commission on Environment and Development (WCED). 1987. *Our Common Future*. New York: Oxford University Press.

World Resources Institute (WRI). 1994–1995. *World Resources Report: A Guide to the Global Environment*. New York: Oxford University Press.

——. 1993. *Country Environmental Studies: An Annotated Bibliography of Environmental and Natural Resource Profiles and Assessments*. Washington, D.C.: World Resources Institute.

Zazueta, Aarón. 1993. "Environmental Challenges in Latin America: Building Organizational Capacities." *Issues in Development*, WRI, July 1993.

——. 1984. *The Mexican State and the Modernization of Agriculture in Caborca, Sonora*. Ph.D. Dissertation, University of California - Davis.

Zazueta, Aarón and Kathleen Courrier. 1994. "In Chiapas, Also Violence to the Environment." *The Houston Chronicle*, 1/26/94.

ORDER FORM

ORDER ADDITIONAL COPIES NOW
and receive a 10% discount

___ YES, please send me ____ copies of **Policy Hits The Ground: Participation and Equity in Environmental Policy-Making** at the special discount price of $13.45, plus $3.50 shipping and handling.

Payment Information:
___ Check enclosed in the amount of: $_____

___ Please charge my credit card:
   ___ Visa   ___ MasterCard

Account Number:_____

Expiration Date: _____

Signature _____

Ship to:

Name: _____

Address: _____

City, State, Zip Code: _____

Daytime Phone: _____

In a hurry? Order by phone with a Visa or MasterCard by calling 1-800-822-0504, or 410-516-6963.

___ Please check here if you would like to receive a complete catalog of WRI publications.

Return this form with payment, to: WRI Publications, P.O. Box 4852, Hampden Station, Baltimore, MD 21211. All orders must be prepaid. Prices subject to change without notice.

World Resources Institute

The World Resources Institute (WRI) is an independent center for policy research and technical assistance on global environmental and development issues. WRI's mission is to move human society to live in ways that protect Earth's environment and its capacity to provide for the needs and aspirations of current and future generations.

Because people are inspired by ideas, empowered by knowledge, and moved to change by greater understanding, the Institute provides—and helps other institutions provide—objective information and practical proposals for policy and institutional change that will foster environmentally sound, socially equitable development. WRI's particular concerns are with globally significant environmental problems and their interaction with economic development and social equity at all levels.

The Institute's current areas of work include economics, forests, biodiversity, climate change, energy, sustainable agriculture, resource and environmental information, trade, technology, national strategies for environmental and resource management, and human health.

In all of its policy research and work with institutions, WRI tries to build bridges between ideas and action, meshing the insights of scientific research, economic and institutional analyses, and practical experience with the need for open and participatory decision-making.

MARSTON SCIENCE LIBRARY

Date Due

Due	Returned	Due	Returned

Renew online @ http://www.uflib.ufl.edu

Select: Renew Books Online / View Account

Loan Policy Information @

http://www.uflib.ufl.edu/as/circ.html